Ministry on th

New Testament patterns of
apostles and apostolic teams
for supporting church plants
and existing churches today.

David Ollerton

***NEWID* books**

Reprinted 2016

ISBN: 978-0-9558397-2-6

Published by *NEWID* books

Cover design by Alan Piper

Printed by Gomer Press
Llandysul, Wales.

Contents

With grateful thanks for
J. Elwyn Davies
1925 - 2007
who inspired this concern

Introduction

These are challenging days for the church in Britain. There are some encouragements in the midst of general decline and a struggle to adjust to a post-modern, pluralist, and very materialistic society where 'truth' is discounted and 'God' is 'all things to all men'.

Some are pessimistic about the church's future, whereas others see it as a day of opportunity and expectation. This book is written for the latter, but hopes to encourage the former. We must always retain an expectation of God's favour and grace towards a Church and a nation that deserve nothing of the sort. He has promised to pour water on the thirsty. In anticipation of such favour we should ask what preparations we should make. As in 2 Kings 3 we have to dig ditches today in expectation of rain tomorrow.

'We must always retain an expectation of God's favour and grace towards a Church and a nation that deserve nothing of the sort'

Large areas of Britain, especially Wales, need to be re-evangelised. In most rural and inner city areas the churches that remain need urgent help, and new church planting will struggle without adequate support. *Waleswide* is an organisation working in Wales to address these issues. Areas of need have been identified, sectors of churches who would work more comfortably together have been recognised, and a number of leaders have begun to give significant time, effort and prayer to seek a new beginning.

The enormity of the task can seem overwhelming, and the temptation is merely to 'tinker on the edges', attempting what circumstances and pragmatics suggest. In considering the way forward it is easy to neglect 'first principles' and just stumble onwards. This book seeks to consider the foundational values for such work. What are the New Testament patterns, justification and mandate for itinerant ministry that seeks to plant and support churches? Who was responsible for planting and supporting churches in the New Testament? How was it done?

It is surprising that for many in the churches in the UK these are neglected questions. We can be so preoccupied with our own church and locality that there is little awareness or sense of responsibility, for mission to our region or nation. Churches often have some plan to contribute in personnel and finance to their immediate locality [their 'Jerusalem' of Acts 1:8], or to adjacent countries [their 'Samaria'] with the advent of budget airlines, and the 'ends of the earth' through missionary links, but not to their own 'back yard' or region [their 'Judea']. There are historical reasons for this. The 'parochial system' and a 'Christendom mindset' can lull us into comfortable assumptions that everywhere else is someone else's responsibility, and that there is probably something happening, but that we just have not heard about it, or don't feel that it is necessarily anything to do with us.

It may also be that we do not think that the New Testament has much to say on the subject. However, through the centuries it is evident that we are prone to a form of blindness when reading the Scriptures. We are prone to see what we think is there, or what fits with our preconceptions or assumed theological preferences. How did Christians for centuries fail to see what the great Reformer Martin Luther saw so clearly, that salvation comes through faith alone? And the 'short-sightedness' did not stop there.

The New Testament speaks of the Gospel being taken from one region to another, using derivatives of the Greek word apostolos ἀπόστολος. However, today ideas of apostles, apostolic teams and an apostolic world vision for mission and church planting are controversial and confused. Have we missed something? Have we made assumptions that have prevented us from making full use of key gifts of Christ for His Church? Can we in the twenty-first century, facing the evangelisation or re-evangelisation of nations, afford to do without what the early church saw as essential?

The issues should be answered, first and foremost, by reference to Biblical text, not theological models. In the past the Evangelical Movement of Wales, for example, has sought to apply this scrutiny : *'We have endeavoured to aim at bringing the principles found in the Scriptures to the fore ...we have not undertaken to include any consideration of developmental factors, which are usually adduced to explain or justify changes in the pattern of church life and practice down through the centuries. We have felt, rather, that it is better and more necessary for us to seek to re-establish the fundamental principles which have become forgotten, neglected or corrupted in the centuries subsequent to apostolic times.'*[1] *'The aim that constantly has been uppermost in our minds has been to reproduce New Testament Christianity in 20th century circumstances... Throughout its history the Church has always been most relevant when it has been most Scriptural...Thus we find ourselves captive to the Word of God. We all of us need to re-examine the encrusted denominational traditions that we have inherited and which we so often perpetuate.'*[2] This is an attempt to apply such scrutiny in the sphere of how churches are planted and strengthened in the twenty-first century.

Those who have looked at the current practice of mission have concluded that *'We are not working in the way the Apostles and those who followed them worked. We may preach the same Gospel, but our methods of work are not the methods they used. The structure of our Church differs greatly from the structure of theirs. Fundamental spiritual principles have been disregarded.'*[3] Others point to our failure to even consider whether a New Testament approach is possible or practicable. They say that since the Church today has hardly attained to the 'whole measure of the fullness of Christ', it can scarcely afford to do without some of the ministry gifts of Christ - apostles, prophets, and evangelists - which they see as still being given to the church, and needed as much today as they were in the first century.'[4]

The issues, therefore, could be vital for the Church in our day. To fail to enquire carefully into what the New Testament actually says on such an important subject would be to do ourselves and the churches a huge disservice. To be guided merely by tradition or current practice is not enough. Being an evangelical is not being able to tick a set of doctrinal boxes only. As Stuart Olyott says, *'It is an instinct. An evangelical on any subject asks 'What does the Bible say?'*[5]

1 'The Ministry and Life of the Christian Church' ; a basis for discussion. Evangelical Movement of Wales 1968 page 4

2 'The Christian Church - a Biblical study' Evangelical Movement of Wales 1966 pages 4 & 5

3 Alex R. Hay 'The New Testament Order for Church and Missionary' : New Testament Missionary Union Argentina 1947, page 18

4 Barney Coombs 'Apostles Today' page 11

5 Noted in personal conversation during a Waleswide Working Group.

Section One

The Place of The Teams

The 'Apostles of the Lamb' and 'Messengers of the churches'

Historical Parallels - Welsh Puritans

Lessons for Today - 1

Chapter One : The 'Apostles of the Lamb' and 'Messengers of the churches'

The word 'apostle', [apóstolos, ἀπόστολος] is used in different ways in the New Testament. Much of the controversy over the subject has arisen from confusing these different usages.

Firstly, it is used in a unique way of the Lord Jesus, *'the apostle and high priest whom we confess' [Hebrews 3:1],* to describe how He was sent by the Father in order to save us. He is the ultimate 'apostle'. All later 'apostles' are 'scaled down versions', reflecting His apostleship in part, to different degrees.

Secondly, it is used of the first twelve disciples, *'these are the names of the twelve apostles: first, Simon (who is called Peter) and his brother Andrew; James son of Zebedee, and his brother John; Philip and Bartholomew; Thomas and Matthew the tax collector; James son of Alphaeus, and Thaddaeus; Simon the Zealot and Judas Iscariot, who betrayed him.' [Matthew 10:2-4].* This number was kept to twelve only. When Judas Iscariot turned apostate he was replaced by Matthias, *'they cast lots, and the lot fell to Matthias; so he was added to the eleven apostles' [Acts 1:26].* The New Testament then recognizes a new 'Twelve', *'so the Twelve gathered all the disciples together' [Acts 6:2],* with no suggestion that the Matthias appointment was a 'uninspired action' or that they should have waited for Paul who was the real 'number 12'. The 'Twelve' were those who had been chosen 'to be with Him', or in Matthias's case to be around Him, during His three years of earthly ministry. These Twelve are afforded a unique place, and their number was not subsequently added to. They were later defined as 'the twelve apostles of the Lamb' [Revelation 21:14].

The 'Twelve' were those who had been chosen "to be with him"

Thirdly, it is used subsequently in a broader sense of others with apostolic ministry. The term 'apostolos' [ἀπόστολος] is used to describe these ministries, and is often translated by Bible translators as 'messenger', 'delegate', or 'representative', to give a different sense than 'the Apostles of the Lamb'. Paul's term 'apostles of the churches' gives a helpful distinction, *'as for Titus, he is my partner and fellow worker among you; as for our brothers, they are representatives of the churches [άπόστολοι έκκλησιών] and an honour to Christ' [2 Corinthians 8:23].* These apostles were gifts of the ascended Christ, given after His ascension, *'but to each one of us grace has been given as Christ apportioned it. This is why it says: 'When he ascended on high, he led captives in his train and gave gifts to men." It was he who gave some to be apostles, some to be prophets, some to be evangelists, and some to be pastors and teachers' [Ephesians 4:7-11].* Initially they would have worked alongside the 'Twelve', who were the special gifts of the ascended Christ receiving their empowering if not their call after the ascension. The 'messengers of the churches' had an apostleship of narrower scope but were also *'to prepare God's people for works of service, so that the body of Christ may be built up' [Ephesians 4:12].* Terry Virgo clarifies the distinction helpfully, *'they were not witnesses of His resurrection but gifts of His ascension'.* [6]

There are at least ten people described as having such an apostolic role, and some see others in Paul's teams and those sent out by him in the same light.

Paul : *'Paul, a servant of Christ Jesus, called to be an apostle and set apart for the gospel of God' [Romans 1:1]*

James [Jesus' natural brother] : *'I went up to Jerusalem to get acquainted with Peter and stayed with him fifteen days. I saw none of the other apostles—only James, the Lord's brother.' [Galatians 1: 18 & 19]*

Barnabas : *'But when the apostles Barnabas and Paul heard of this, they tore their clothes and rushed out into the crowd' [Acts 14:14].*

Apollos : *'Now, brothers, I have applied these things to myself and Apollos for your benefit.... For it seems to me that God has put us apostles on display at the end of the procession, like men condemned to die in the arena' [1 Corinthians 4:6-9].*

Andronicus and **Junias** : *'Greet Andronicus and Junias, my relatives who have been in prison with me. They are outstanding among the apostles, and they were in Christ before I was' [Romans 16:7].* [Much has been made of the fact that 'Junias' was a female name, but the gender is inconclusive as it is found in that period as a male and a female name.]

Epaphroditus : *'But I think it is necessary to send back to you Epaphroditus, my brother, fellow worker and fellow soldier, who is also your messenger [ἀποστολος], whom you sent to take care of my needs' [Philippians 2:25].*

6 Terry Virgo in Newfrontiers Magazine Volume 2 - Issue 04 - September-November 2003 page 8

Titus : *'As for Titus, he is my partner and fellow worker among you; as for our brothers, they are representatives [ἀποστολοι] of the churches and an honour to Christ [2 Corinthians 8:23].*

One unnamed : *'we are sending along with him the brother who is praised by all the churches for his service to the gospel... they are representatives of the churches' [2 Corinthians 8: 18-23].*

Timothy and **Silas** : *'Paul, Silas and Timothy, To the church of the Thessalonians in God the Father and the Lord Jesus Christ:...as apostles of Christ we could have been a burden to you' [1 Thessalonians 1:1-2:6].*

Fourthly, there are those designated 'false apostles', *'but I do not think I am in the least inferior to those 'super-apostles'... For such men are false apostles, deceitful workmen, masquerading as apostles of Christ' [2 Corinthians 5:5-13].* The false apostles are set in contrast to the ongoing ministry of those who are genuine.

These 'apostles of the churches' did not satisfy the qualification of having been a personal witness of Christ's Resurrection who had *'been with us the whole time the Lord Jesus went in and out among us, beginning from John's baptism to the time when Jesus was taken up from us' [Acts 1 : 21&22].* Paul's claim to have seen the Lord later, *'last of all he appeared to me also, as to one abnormally born' [1 Corinthians 15:7&8]* was not a claim for him to be put alongside the 'Twelve' any more than the hundreds who saw the Galilee resurrection appearances. Paul's apostolic call and ministry to the Gentiles was, however, wholly accepted and affirmed by the Twelve in Jerusalem : *'For God, who was at work in the ministry of Peter as an apostle to the Jews, was also at work in my ministry as an apostle to the Gentiles. James, Peter and John, those reputed to be pillars, gave me and Barnabas the right hand of fellowship when they recognized the grace given to me' [Galatians 2: 8&9].* Some 'apostles of the churches', particularly Paul and Banabas, showed evidence of *'the things that mark an apostle—signs, wonders and miracles—were done among you with great perseverance' [2 Corinthians 12:12].* This was integral to breaking new ground in a pagan context, *'they listened to Barnabas and Paul telling about the miraculous signs and wonders God had done among the Gentiles through them' [Acts 15:12],* and could be so today.

The existence of itinerant 'messengers of the churches' is spoken of in the writings of the early Church outside the canonical Scriptures, especially in the Shepherd of Hermas and the Didache[7]. Origen and Eusebius speak of itinerant evangelists in the second century *'there were still many evangelists of the Word eager to use their inspired zeal after the example of the apostles for the increase and building up of the divine Word'.*[8] However, the practice was soon phased out as the churches became more and more centralized and institutionalized.

By the time of the Reformation a contrary view of the ongoing ministry of apostles had developed. It was argued that what was done in the Acts of the Apostles was in some way 'formative, but not normative', and so does not have a contemporary relevance. The Reformers tended to emphasize the temporary nature of the second category of Apostles, without due consideration of the ongoing nature of the other three. They said that the ministries of apostle, prophet and evangelist were temporary provisions for the first century only, and that only the roles of pastor and teacher had permanence. They held this view for a number of reasons. The Roman Catholic Church had taught a doctrine of 'apostolic succession' that led to an ongoing papacy that could redefine truth or add to the Scriptural foundations of the ***'apostles' doctrine'** [Acts 2:42]* that had been ***'once for all entrusted to the saints'** [Jude 1:3]*. In order to counter this position, and to make it clear that the content of the New Testament was not to be added to, it was argued that the 'apostles', meaning the twelve 'Apostles of the Lamb', had been responsible for writing the New Testament. As a result their deaths ensured no more new inspired and authoritative truth could be added. It is not a particularly good argument, however, as most of the Twelve did not write Scripture, and some of the others who did [Mark, Luke, Paul, James, Jude, and the writer to the Hebrews] had very tenuous links to the Twelve. The authority and inerrancy of the Scripture rests on the better testimony of each Person of the Triune God who inspired it, and its own testimony, truthfulness and reliability.

However, the view held, and has been assumed in most, though not all, of Protestantism ever since. To many of the Reformed tradition any form of apostolic ministry, and the accompanying miraculous, was for the early Church only. Walter Chantry has no doubt that the role of apostle has ceased: *'The Book of Revelation is the last apostolic word to the church'* [9], *'the*

7 Shepherd of Hermas Vis. 3.5.1, Sim. 9.15.4, 16.5 Quoted in Michael Green 'Evangelism in the Early Church' page 168

8 Eusebius 'Ecclesiastical History' 5.10.2 Quoted in Michael Green 'Evangelism in the Early Church' page 169

9 Walter Chantry 'Signs of the Apostles' page 37

apostles are dead'[10], *'George Whitefield ... renounced all pretences to the extraordinary powers and signs of apostleship, peculiar to the age of inspiration, and extinct with them.'*[11] W.G.T. Shedd, quoting B. B. Warfield, makes it clear that there were Apostles, an Apostolic Church, and an Apostolic Age but that *'they were part of the credentials of the Apostles as the authoritative agents of God in founding the church. Their function thus confined them to distinctively the Apostolic Church and they necessarily passed away with it.'*[12] John Kennedy states that *'the ministry of apostleship and prophecy as embodied in particular people was but a temporary expedient. It was vitally necessary during the transition period when the written Word was being formulated...but the written Word completed, the particular ministry of the apostle and prophet became redundant, just as the observation of the Old Testament sacrifices had to give way to their fulfilment in Christ'.*[13] Dr Martyn Lloyd Jones in describing the ongoing nature of ministry said that *'in the first group, the extraordinary and temporary, we have apostles and prophets and evangelists; and in the second permanent group we have pastors and teachers'.*[14]

Tragically, the effect is that we do not even attempt to do things in a New Testament way, and our expectations are shaped as a result.

But on what Biblical basis, from New Testament text, can such assumptions be made, and what is the consequence of such a view? Such distinctions and limits on permanence cannot be drawn from the New Testament. According to O. Palmer Robertson the most that can be said is that *'nothing in Scripture explicitly indicates that the apostolate ever would come to an end. Yet it is generally recognized that no one in the church today functions with the authority of the original apostles'.*[15]

It is the consequences for mission at home and abroad that result from such views that are of concern. Tragically, the effect is that we do not even attempt to do things in a New Testament way, and our expectations are shaped as a result. The great Puritan John Owen perhaps stated the practical

10 Ibid page 59

11 Ibid page 143

12 Ibid page 145 & 146 quoting Warfield in 'Counterfeit Miracles'

13 John Kennedy 'The Torch and the Testimony' page 30

14 D Martyn Lloyd-Jones 'Christian Unity: An Exposition of Ephesians 4:1 to 16'. Banner of Truth. 1980

15 O. Palmer Robertson 'The Final Word : A Biblical Response to the Case for Tongues and Prophecy Today. Banner of Truth page 80

consequences most starkly when he concluded that *'no church whatever hath power to ordain men ministers for the conversion of infidels. Since the cessation of extraordinary officers the case of that work is devolved merely on the providence of God, being left without the verge of church institutions.'*[16] As a result mission was restricted to the local and for the most part the church had to wait a hundred years before New Testament practice began to be rediscovered by the Moravians and William Carey.

The Reformers of the sixteenth century got much right, but they too were people of their own age, with their own blinkers. Many of our assumptions about 'New Testament Teams' have been inherited from this period, and should be re-examined. Patterns of clericalism, modes of baptism, rites, and Christendom ideas that gave a lack of missionary perspective were generally assumed, not challenged. Tertullian [c. AD 160-215] had said that *'custom without truth is error grown cold.'*[17]

However, not all were convinced by this view, especially among Reformed Baptists. Both the General and Particular Baptists of the later Puritan era set apart gifted men to evangelise and plant churches, calling them 'messengers'. Thomas Grantham (1633/4-1692), a General Baptist minister from Boston, Lincolnshire, pastored churches from 1652, but in 1666 he was appointed 'messenger', founding churches in Lincolnshire, Norfolk, Warwickshire, and other counties, giving ongoing oversight and care to the churches. He said, *'God hath given to his church ... a travelling ministry [messengers or apostles], unfixed in respect of particular societies [churches] to take all occasions to cause the light of the glorious gospel to shine unto such as sit in darkness, to plant churches or settle them in the faith, to visit and comfort those who have believed through grace.'*[18] In a sermon preached in Boston on December 12th, 1773 on the occasion of the commissioning of three missionaries to preach the Gospel among the Indians Thomas Prince took issue with the then current view. He argued that the New Testament distinguishes not so much between temporary and permanent ministries, as between localised and itinerant ministries. *'So long as there are heathens to be evangelised, to be converted to the Christian Faith, to be baptised and gathered into Churches; so long do both the Kingdom of Christ and necessities of men*

16 John Owen Works XVI page 93 Quoted by David Kingdon in his paper 'Church Planting in the New Testament' section 4.4

17 Alex R. Hay Op.cit page 285

18 Thomas Grantham 'The Successors of the Apostles' 1674 Quoted by Richard Haydon-Knowell in 'Restoration' Magazine Sept. 1985

require the office [of apostle/messenger or evangelist], as well as in the Primitive Times.' [19]

Few would disagree that the Church today needs a return to New Testament order and fruitfulness. If there are no longer 'Apostles of the Lamb' operating that does not preclude the apostolic ministry of 'apostles of the churches'. Kevin J. Connor describes them as *'apostles of lesser order and grace.'* [20] Bernard Lewis says *'in considering the New Testament use of "apostle"... there is a pattern of completion and continuation in the groups and individuals who were so described. In this completion-continuation tension we want to suggest that as one set of apostles completed a recognised responsibility they then commissioned others to continue a more general element e.g. the preaching of the Word of God and/or church planting.'* [21] Even John Calvin suggests something of the same, *'those functions were not instituted in the church to be perpetual, but only to endure so long as churches were to be formed where none previously existed ... although I deny not that afterward God occasionally raised up Apostles, or at least Evangelists in their stead, as has been done in our time.'* [22] David Kingdon puts the issue in clear focus, *'the distinction of ministries in the New Testament is not between temporary and permanent officers, as the Reformed tradition has generally maintained, but between peripatetic and localised ministries. Apostles and evangelists, and probably in some instances prophets and teachers, exercised a peripatetic ministry directed to the planting of churches. Elders and deacons as well as teachers and prophets, exercised their ministry within the local church.'* [23] Arthur Wallis distinguished them as *'men on the spot' and 'men on the move'.* [24] Others would suggest that not even pastors and teachers, and certainly not prophets, were entirely located within a local church, being called to equip the saints in pastoring and teaching in the wider sphere as well. The pastoring and teaching would be

Few would disagree that the Church today needs to return to New Testament order and fruitfulness.

19 R Pierce Bearer 'Pioneers in Mission' Eerdmans 1966 page 70. Quoted by David Kingdon section 1:1

20 Kevin J Connor The Church in the New Testament page 145

21 Bernard Lewis's MA thesis 'So I Send You' University of Wales Lampeter. 2004

22 John Calvin 'Institutes of Religion' IV.III.4

23 David Kingdon in his paper for the 1974 Carey Ministers Conference 'Church Planting in the New Testament' section 4:2

24 Arthur Wallis Restoration Magazine September / October 1985 page 2

done by the elders, and one in particular, ***'the elders who direct the affairs of the church well are worthy of double honour, especially those whose work is preaching and teaching' [1 Timothy 5:17]***. There is no 'Pastor Barnabas of Antioch, Pastor John of Ephesus, Pastor Titus of Crete...'. It is an interesting fact that the New Testament nowhere refers to one pastor of a local church.

In the light of the issues at stake David Kingdon gives a stern warning. *'It is, I believe, vitally important that at this juncture we apply the Reformation principle of 'Sola Scriptura' with the utmost rigour. To say, or think 'Sola Scriptura' plus the received interpretation of Calvin and Owen is, in fact, to deny the 'Sola Scriptural principle'.*[25]

He goes on to challenge us with the implications of these distinctions : *'The missionary obligation of the church must be reflected in the structure of the church. The missionary obligation of the Church at Antioch found expression in the sending forth of Saul and Barnabas, and their sending forth was a continual reminder of its missionary obligation. Now we must not impose our pattern of organization upon the New Testament at this point. Even if Saul and Barnabas had only planted a Church in the next city they would still have been fulfilling the church's missionary obligation. Planting the Gospel in the next town to our Church today is as much an expression of the Church's missionary obligation as is sending a missionary to plant a church in a foreign country. The man who is sent to the next locality is no less an 'apostolos' than the man who is sent thousands of miles away. But do our Churches realise this, and do their structures reflect this? I very much doubt whether they do'.* [26]

25 David Kingdon Op.cit section 1:4

26 David Kingdon Op.cit section 4:6

Chapter Two : Historical Parallels - Welsh Puritans

The principles for church life, growth and leadership set out in the New Testament are timeless in their relevance. Therefore, where they have been practised in subsequent centuries it is possible to see benefits similar, though not on the same scale, to those so evident in the first century. This is certainly true in seasons when new churches were planted or existing ones strengthened through the input of travelling ministry and teams. They brought the benefits of experience, insight and specific gifts to situations that needed them

This book has been written in Wales but no narrowing of scope and application is intended. Wales is a small country with a rich history of church growth and seasons when the whole land was profoundly affected by fresh initiatives of the Spirit of God. Its history, therefore, offers a microcosm that shows patterns in a relatively small sphere and, because of its distinct language, was somewhat immune from wider trends. Periods from its history, therefore, serve us well by way of illustration though parallels from England will also be referred to.

The situation at the beginning of the twenty-first century is one in which large parts of inner-city, formerly industrial, and rural areas are in great need of new church plants or the strengthening of what remains. Such a situation is not new in Wales, and the role of teams and itinerant ministry as outlined in the previous chapter has been crucial in the past. In fact, when the nation needed to be evangelized, or re-evangelised, it is difficult to find a time when such teams did not play the decisive role. What can be known of the coming of Celtic Christianity to Wales reveals an effective itinerant ministry. If most of the church foundations in West and South Wales bearing the name of 'David' were founded by the Patron Saint then he was a prolific and mobile church planter with an extensive team.

What can be known of the coming of Celtic Christianity to Wales reveals an effective itinerant ministry.

Centuries of superstition and the 'Dark Ages' followed, with the Reformation of the sixteenth century having comparatively little effect in Wales. In practice Wales remained a largely Catholic land, with a liberal mixture of folk religion and superstition from pre-Christian centuries. By the mid-1600s, therefore, Wales was in urgent need of new churches or transitions, and the same was largely true before the coming of the Methodists in the 1730s. The seasons of revival from the early 1820s to 1904 were among a population in which evangelism and Christian education had produced something of an attentive audience, where churches existed in a nominally Christian population. That is not the situation today, so it is to the Puritans of the seventeenth century that we turn for encouragement. They challenged the institutional and formal practices of their day, calling for a more Biblical and dynamic church.

John Miles [1621-1684] was the founder of the Baptist Church at Ilston on Gower, near Swansea, which led to the founding of others across South Wales. He was born in what was then a Welsh speaking part of Herefordshire, and after leaving Brasenose College, Oxford, in 1636, came to South Wales. He may have served in the Parliamentary army sent to restore order in the area in 1648. In the summer of 1649 he and a colleague, Thomas Proud, travelled to London and attended the Glass House, the leading Baptist church in the capital. They arrived *'immediately after our brethren there had kept a day to seek the Lord that he would send labourers into the dark corners and parts of this land'.*[27] Presumably, they were then baptised as believers before being promptly sent back to South Wales as 'messengers', along the same lines as Thomas Grantham had been in Lincolnshire, to gather a *'company or society of people holding forth and practising the doctrine, worship, order and discipline of the Gospel according to the primitive institution'.*[28]

The 1640s were a time of upheaval as Cromwell's successes in the Civil War introduced a short season of 'freedom', in church life, with the monopoly of Anglicanism being swept away. In 1649 John Miles was appointed as rector of St. Illtyd's Parish Church in Ilston, despite being a Baptist. After a slow start by October 1650 the Ilston Baptists numbered 43 and by the end of that year Miles had baptised his fiftieth member. By 1660 there were 250 drawn from all over Gower and beyond.

Initially, the members gathered at Ilston, but due to the distances and poor roads they were then encouraged to meet in homes in their own areas on

27 B.R.White 'John Miles and the Structures of the Calvinistic Baptist Mission to South Wales 1649-1660' in 'Welsh Baptist Studies' page 36

28 Ilston Churchbook MS in 'Welsh Baptist Studies' page 36

some Sundays and mid-week nights. On other Sundays they all gathered together. Leaders were appointed for the scattered areas including Swansea, Neath, and Aberavon, and eventually most of these developed into churches in their own right. They were followed by others at Hay on Wye and Llanharan in 1650, at Carmarthen in 1651 and at Abergavenny in 1652, with other contacts developing in Gelligaer, Llangeinor, Glyncorrwg and elsewhere.

The churches were kept closely connected by visits from Miles and others, circular letters, and by gathering and training potential leaders. The elders and *'messengers.'* [29] from the churches also gathered to discuss points of difficulty or dispute and to maintain overall discipline. Between 1650 and 1656 at least seven such 'General Meetings' were held, the first at Ilston on 6th and 7th November, 1650, where among other things they made joint plans, *'to carry on the work in Wales'.*

In all this period John Miles travelled to support the emerging churches, drawing in others to help, including David Davies, the 'Baptist' vicar of Gelligaer. Others were sent out as 'messengers' for a wider ministry of preaching, but also to spend extended periods with other churches to help them develop. Walter Prosser from Hay spent weeks in Carmarthen when the church there was first started, his expenses and salary of £32 per annum paid by the other churches. William Thomas also came to help for one week in three.[30]

This whole system of cooperation between churches to release ministry out from the churches was very fruitful, despite inevitable tensions. It represented a move from 'independency' to 'interdependency', and it prospered until the season of opportunity ended in 1662 when all 'nonconformist' ministers were turned out of their churches. With the onset of persecution, when the monarchy was restored under Charles II, Miles emigrated to the new state of Massachusetts to start all over again.

---

29 B.R.White Op.cit page 70

30 B.R.White Op.cit page 54 & 58

Stephen Hughes [1622 - 1688] was the son of a Carmarthen silk merchant who was appointed minister of the parish of Meidrim in 1655. He was a Congregationalist in an Anglican building until, like John Miles, his ministry was brought to a sudden end when he was 'ejected' in 1662 with the introduction of various forms of persecution.

He married *'a pious woman in Swanzey, whose portion, frugality, and industry contributed much to his comfortable subsistence and future usefulness',*[31] and though living in Swansea continued to preach across Carmarthenshire. His wife's social status, and respect for his preaching, brought him some protection from the laws banning nonconformist preaching. He travelled continuously despite the restrictions of the 'Penal Code' preaching, *'in the darkest corners, and in places where the people had ignorant readers that could not preach. His moderation and lively preaching recommended him to the esteem of the sober part of the Gentry, by whose connivance he often preached in the public churches, which were much thronged by the vast numbers that came to hear him'.*[32] When the laws were relaxed under the 'Indulgences' of 1672 he started licensing his house in Swansea as a church, together with others in Pencader and Llanstephan, and then got the job of giving out the licenses and so got his friends to do the same. The Bishop was enraged by how he used and bent the rules, even, *'intruding himself into churches'* to preach.[33] As a result he was always in fear of arrest, a fate which at last caught up with him when he was imprisoned in Carmarthen, *'to the prejudice of his health and hazard of his life'.*[34]

He was excommunicated for 'keeping school' in Swansea,[35] a common practice among his peers for developing a new generation of leaders, twelve being ordained in the year of his death. In addition to this he published about twenty books in Welsh, some of which ran into several editions, despite English opposition to the language. With help from various sources, including Anglican, he also published 8,000 copies of the Welsh Bible of which he gave away 1,000 to the poor.

31 Edmund Calamy's 'Ejected Ministers' page 718

32 Edmund Calamy Op.cit page 718

33 Thomas Richards 'Wales under the Indulgence'. Page 122

34 Edmund Calamy Op.cit page 718

35 Thomas Richards 'Wales under the Penal Code' page 39

His tireless travels all over Carmarthenshire and into south Cardiganshire, led to the founding of new churches at Carmarthen, Capel Isaac, Henllan, Pantteg, Pencader, Llanybri, Llanedi and Trelech, to which he then gave oversight. Most of the later Congregational churches in the county were then planted by those founded by him.

For this work of founding and overseeing churches, training and involving other leaders, and gathering resources he was known, perhaps rightly, as the 'Apostle of Carmarthenshire'.

Huw Owen, Bronclydwr [1639 -1700] lived in a remoter part of North Wales around Barmouth, so less is known of him. His contemporary described him thus : *'His preaching was affectionate and moving and many were wrought upon by it. He was a burning and shining light in an obscure corner of the world. A bright star that moved in a large orb.'*[36]

He was at Oxford preparing for ministry when the 'Penal Code' of 1662, the laws persecuting nonconformists, came into force and so he returned to Gwynedd. According to Edmund Calamy, writing in 1713, he *'lived upon a little estate of his own there [Bronclydwr] and preached the Gospel to the poor ignorant people without taking anything of them...He went about preaching the Gospel of Salvation, through that and the Neighbouring Counties of Montgomery; and sometimes stepped into Carnarvonshire, and other parts. He had five or six places where he used to preach in Merionethshire, and some of them twenty miles distant from him. He had near as many in Montgomeryshire, of which some were about thirty miles from his habitation. He performed his circuit in about three months time, and then began again. Great numbers of people attended his ministry, and were much affected with it. He laboured indefatigably, and much impaired his health, by riding often in the night, and cold rains over the mountains... He was a primitive apostolical Christian."*[37]

He was ordained in Wrexham, 'to care for the Independents of Meirion, to gather together the few Independents in the county, to preach to them, and to teach them the things of the Gospel.'[38] This he did, initially by gathering a

36 Edmund Calamy Op.cit page 710

37 Edmund Calamy Op.cit page 710

38 D.D.Jones 'Eglwys Meirion a Hugh Owen in 'Eglwysi'r Annibywyr' page 64

church one Sunday in Bronclydwr, next in Dolgellau, and then Bala and Llanuwchllyn. By 1715 the groups in Bronclydwr, Dolgellau and Bala still only numbered 150 in total, but the Independent churches of the next century in three counties traced their origins to the foundations he laid in many small groups over a vast area. When the persecutions eased after the 'Declaration of Indulgence' he, like Stephen Hughes, applied for licenses to start churches in homes across the area, in Bodwenni near Bala, Cynfal near Trawsfynydd, Erwgoyel near Dolgellau, Peniarth near Llanfihangel y Pennant, and in his own house at Llanegryn.

He preached, taught, trained, and laid foundations through relentless travelling. For this he was known as the 'Father of the Arfon Independants' before his sphere widened still farther, after which he was the 'Apostol y Gogledd', the 'Apostle of the North'.

Chapter Three : Lessons for Today - 1

If principles of truth are clear in the New Testament they will be equally applicable in any century, whether the Seventeenth or the Twenty-First. If itinerant 'messengers of the churches' worked in teams to plant and develop churches, alongside and after the work of the twelve 'Apostles of the Lamb', then the principles and patterns exhibited will be essential to fruitfulness and extension in any age or culture, including hopefully our own. If *'the apostles and their helpers are pioneers through the Spirit's power; founding and establishing the Church of Christ,'*[39] then we can scarcely do with anything less today. There are dangers and excesses, of course, but they should not be allowed to deflect the church from essential elements of its mission.

Bernard Lewis points to another issue that has led to caution : *'I am conscious that to use the terms apostles, apostolic or related terms when discussing approaches to Christian ministry or mission may in itself be provocative ...One's orthodoxy or heterodoxy can in some quarters be determined by the use or rejection of the apostolic terms. It is therefore with a measure of caution that this question is actually raised. ...I raise it however because of a recognised need in many areas and in the hope of enhancing the ministry of the church (or churches) in others.'*[40] The practical consequences are enormous, and as mentioned earlier, the issues should be decided on the basis of biblical exegesis, not historical theology or pragmatics.

A local church's responsibility in mission means that it cannot live independently of others, or oblivious, or indifferent to the needs of the region, nation or nations beyond it. Churches should embrace the responsibility for un-evangelised and un-churched parts of their nation, and for the needy areas and churches within it. If leaders of a local church are only pastoring their own people, encouraging their people to attend their own church's activities, or to connect to the community of their own church they cannot be said to be fully New Testament in practice. New Testament churches were planted with a spiritual DNA that also looked to needs beyond their immediate boundaries.

39 'The Ministry and Life of the Christian Church' Op.cit page 17

40 Bernard Lewis Op.cit

Kevin Connor[41] has contrasted the ethos of the church in Jerusalem to that in Antioch. He describes the first as tending to a restricted Judaistic spirit, so as to keep things centralized round Jerusalem. It produced a measure of insularity, sectarianism and even pride. The church in Antioch, however, was prepared to be outward looking, taking risks, sending its best leaders, getting its vision and direction from the Holy Spirit, and initiating a mission to nations. Sadly, the Jerusalem spirit can still be with us. It can almost become part of a church's DNA. We have much to learn from Antioch if our nation, and the nations, are to be 're-churched' once more.

The lessons to be taken on board are clear enough, will certainly be challenging, and will require a re-orientation of what it means to be a local church, or in local church ministry. Without any order of priority they can be set out as follows :

- Local churches, and especially their leaders, should take on board a clear responsibility for their mission to their region and nation, as well as the nations.
- Churches should be responsible for recognizing an individual's ministry and call to a wider role, testing that call, sending, possibly supporting, and being a point of accountability. We should recognize ministry called to be 'on the move' as well as 'on the spot'.
- Antioch does not seem to have funded Paul and Barnabas. They received support from churches they had previously founded [Philippians 4:14-17], but there is no record of dependence on, or even support from Antioch.
- Some of the larger growing churches could consider releasing their best men as Antioch did. To lose Paul and Barnabas at such a critical time could not have been an easy decision. It should have come down to call, vision and obedience.
- Those called to ministry and leadership should consider their contribution to the wider needs. For some it will require acknowledging a personal call to the wider, not the local, to be 'on the move' after having previously ministered 'on the spot'. Such leaders will probably have years of experience behind them, and such a change will call for real inconvenience and sacrifice. It may involve 'tent making' initially or in part, i.e. taking some secular employment if circumstances require it. ***'Paul***

41 Kevin J. Connor 'The Vision of an Antioch Church' pages 14 - 6

went to see them, and because he was a tentmaker as they were, he stayed and worked with them' [Acts 18:3]. It could certainly mean long hours, stepping out of comfort zones, and much travel. People who have been used to large jobs, churches and profiles will need to be content to work in small places with small resources, but huge potential.

- Those travelling should gather a team to travel with them, or on their behalf. Such a team would need to be made up of a variety of gifts, with a constant 'through-put' of younger people learning on the job. The concept of 'teams' will be explored in the next section.
- The personnel in teams in the New Testament were not permanent. People joined and left regularly, or worked out from the team. If the area being served is within the same region, or a smaller nation, the team members would not need to be full-time or permanently travelling together. They could be drawn regularly from different churches for shorter periods to serve a local church or area. Equally, for convenience, much use could be made of mobile phones, conference calls, internet blogs, or places to gather leaders together for training, development and general input from the team, though this would be no substitute to regular working in the particular local church.
- Churches should give the same recognition and priority to ministry 'on the move' as to *'ministry on the spot'*. Resources of people, time, money and especially training should be given to both. The church at Lystra recommended and released the young Timothy to join Paul's team. They were clearly willing to invest someone with real potential into the wider work. ***'He came to Derbe and then to Lystra, where a disciple named Timothy lived, whose mother was a Jewess and a believer, but whose father was a Greek. The brothers at Lystra and Iconium spoke well of him' [Acts 16:1&2].***
- The church should have realistic expectations of their 'messengers'. They are 'lesser apostles' at most. Unlike the 'Twelve', and even Paul, *'present-day apostles: 1. Do not write Scripture. 2. Do not experience the appearance of the Risen Lord. 3. Do not enjoy an unparalleled revelation of the gospel. 4. Do not wield Paul's spiritual power. 5. Do not enjoy spiritual experiences on the magnitude of trips to the Third Heaven.'* [42] At the opposite end of the scale, the 'messengers' are a far cry from the figures of church tradition. Barney Coombes quotes W.F.P. Burton who

42 Dave Harvey 'Polity : Serving and Leading the Local Church'. Sovereign Grace Perspectives page 18.

helped to plant nearly 1,500 churches in the Democratic Republic of the Congo : '*When as a little boy I was taken to church, there was a coloured window in the end of the building showing the twelve apostles. They were dressed in most elaborately decorated robes, and carried croziers, orbs, lambs and other unnatural symbols in their hands, while round their heads were great halos, something like Lancashire cheeses. I sat looking at that window Sunday after Sunday, until I really thought that apostles were like that - but they were not. It was sheer imagination. Let me give you a Bible picture of an apostle: He is a weak little chap with a poor voice (2 Corinthians 10:10), a jailbird (Acts 16:23). He looks undernourished and his clothing is disreputable (1 Corinthians 4:11). If you look at his hands, they are stained and cracked by the hard work of softening skins and sewing them into tents, for that is his livelihood (Acts 18:3). At times he is very ill, even despairing of life (2 Corinthians 1:8-11; Galatians 4:13; 2 Corinthians 11:30). Perhaps these infirmities have come from the terrible sufferings which he has undergone (2 Corinthians 11:23-28). That picture has not much in common with the twelve complacent old gentlemen looking benignly at one from the church window, has it! The apostles whom Christ gives to the church are neither rogues nor super-saints. They are not relics of church history or figments of someone's imagination. They are men called of God to a particular ministry - a ministry that has been foundational to the church of the past and that will be essential to the church of the future.*'[43]

- It could also be said that neither were they celebrities, pastors of large churches, denominational heads or those who sold most books or spoke at international conferences. There is a trend in some contemporary models of apostolic ministry for a dependence on pragmatics and marketing rather than patterns discernible in the New Testament. The former may do some good in as much as it seeks to address a need for a 'ministry on the move', and will certainly be better than no model at all, but a model based on Scripture must do much better.

43 Barney Coombs Op.cit page 13

Section Two

The Purpose of The Teams

Chapter Four : The Work of the Teams

Jesus did not send out his disciples on their own, but in pairs. When Paul travelled he was almost invariably accompanied by others. Leadership in the New Testament, for those who travelled or those who were elders of local churches, was always plural. The word 'Team' is used to describe a committed band that worked together to plant and strengthen churches. They were relational in nature, showing no traces of rank or of having ecclesiastical authority over churches. Theirs was a spiritual ministry, authority and purpose.

Jesus sent out the twelve. They went on his behalf as if it were he that was going.

Jesus prepared the Twelve, the 'Apostles of the Lamb', during his three years of public ministry. He taught them, discipled them by close questioning and accountability, modelled what ministry meant, and then sent them out, two by two, to do the same public work as He was doing. *'These twelve Jesus sent out with the following instructions: "... As you go, preach this message: `The kingdom of heaven is near.' Heal the sick, raise the dead, cleanse those who have leprosy, drive out demons. Freely you have received, freely give' [Matthew 10:5-8]*. Later He sent out a further seventy-two, *'two by two ahead of him to every town and place where he was about to go. He told them, "The harvest is plentiful, but the workers are few. Ask the Lord of the harvest, therefore, to send out workers into his harvest field. Go! I am sending you out like lambs among wolves..." He who listens to you listens to me; he who rejects you rejects me; but he who rejects me rejects him who sent me'. [Luke 10 : 1-3&16]*. They went on His behalf, as if it were He who was going. We do not know how many of the 'Seventy-two' were later scattered from Jerusalem into the nations, or whether any became part of Paul's teams as 'messengers of the churches'. It would have been ideal training if they had.

The Twelve stayed in Jerusalem initially, despite the persecution following Stephen's death : *'On that day a great persecution broke out against the church at Jerusalem, and all except the apostles were scattered throughout Judea and Samaria' [Acts 8:1]*. Apart from John being on Patmos and Peter's apostolic sphere *'as an apostle to the Jews' [Galatians 2:8]*, little is known of what happened to the other ten. The so-called *'Acts of Thomas'* says they drew lots to decide which parts of the world they would go to. *'Thomas obtained by lot Parthia, Andrew Scythia, John Asia...but Peter seems to have preached to the Jews of the dispersion in Pontus and Galatia, Bithynia, Cappadocia and Asia, and in the end he came to Rome. These same Acts of Thomas maintain that ...Thomas went to India. Although the evidence is late, it may well be true. Pantaenus also is reputed to have gone to India and to have found Christians there before him, who were rejoicing in the original Hebrew of St Matthew's Gospel left to them by another apostolic figure, St Bartholomew!'* [44] Tradition also has it that Philip went to Carthage; Matthew to Persia, Egypt and Ethiopia; Matthias to Syria; Simon the Zealot and Judas / Thaddeus to Britain...[45] but myth spins a misleading web! It will be safer to focus on the New Testament which is profitable for our instruction so we can be thoroughly equipped for every good work.

The 'Twelve' and the 'messengers' were essentially 'sent ones'. They were people with a call and commission to 'go'. The word 'apóstolos, ἀπόστολος,' literally means a person sent, an envoy, a messenger, a representative, closely associated with the 'sender'. In everyday Greek use it was used of a commander of a naval expedition, a band of colonists sent overseas, or of an ambassador[46]. Paul described himself as ***'an ambassador in chains' [Ephesians 6:20]*** and a ***'prisoner of Christ Jesus for the sake of you Gentiles' [Ephesians 3:1]***, seeing his circumstances as directly related to the One Who sent him. ***'We are therefore Christ's ambassadors, as though God were making his appeal through us' [2 Corinthians 5:20]***. They were not sent essentially by a church, a members' meeting, a council or a Missionary Board. *'A majority vote cannot decide as to who have been chosen'.*[47] *'Neither Timothy nor Titus had the freedom to develop their own ministry statements. They were men under the authority of another, but in their places of ministry they, like Paul himself, were not bound by the sending elders.'* [48]

The nature of what they were sent to do was multi-faceted. Initially, it was evangelistic, they were bearers of the Gospel. *'Apostles exist for the Gospel. They are sent forth to preserve and proclaim its glorious message'.*[49] However, they were not merely evangelists. They proclaimed the Gospel to

44 Michael Green 'Evangelism in the Early Church' page 166

45 Frank Viola 'The Untold Story of the New Testament Church' page 173

46 Dictionary of New Testament Theology vol. 1 page 127

47 Alex R. Hay Op.cit page 305

48 Bernard Lewis Op.cit

49 Dave Harvey Op.cit page 20

make disciples, to establish churches that they cared for, develop leaders to oversee the new church, and then move on to repeat the process:

Some writers, in their eagerness to avoid the word 'apostle', and thereby imply an exact continuation of the ministry of the 'Twelve' have chosen to describe the 'messengers' as evangelists or church-planters only, or in the case of Alex Hay, to completely confuse the two. He claimed that the terms `apostle' and `evangelist', were interchangeable descriptive titles for the same people, the former as messengers of churches and the latter as propagators of the Gospel. He claimed that not to change to using only the term evangelist would have been confusing.[50] Confusing indeed! Others have equated all Paul's team members, the 'messengers', with evangelists.[51] There is no evidence for such a link, though no doubt some members of the team would have the evangelistic gift and so bring its benefit to all. Timothy is exhorted to do the work of an evangelist even though it may not have been his primary gift, ***'endure hardship, do the work of an evangelist, discharge all the duties of your ministry'*** *[2 Timothy 4:5]*, and Ephesians 4:11 clearly distinguishes the two gifts, ***'it was he who gave some to be apostles, some to be prophets, some to be evangelists, and some to be pastors and teachers'.***

Apostolic input to a local church would keep their focus looking outward not inward.

All the *'Seventy-two'* were sent by Jesus, but that did not make them all 'apostles'. Paul preached the Gospel, but that did not make him primarily an evangelist. He never used the term 'evangelist' of himself. It was only used of Philip [Acts 21:8] and indirectly of Timothy [2 Timothy 4:5]. However, he certainly saw 'preaching the Gospel' [ἐυαγγελίζομαι - the verb of the noun] as central to what he did: ***'for Christ did not send me to baptize, but to preach the gospel'*** *[1 Corinthians 1:17]*, ***'yet when I preach the gospel, I cannot boast, for I am compelled to preach. Woe to me if I do not preach the gospel!'*** *[1 Corinthians 9:16]*. Any role, gift or ministry that can be remotely associated with the 'apostolic' should be Gospel-centred. Apostolic input to a local church would keep their focus looking outward not inward, and it would *'ensure that the gospel is preached and applied in the daily life of the church'.*[52]

50 Alex R. Hay Op.cit pages 223, 229-33

51 'The Ministry and Life of the Christian Church' Op.cit page 15

52 Dave Harvey Op.cit page 20

This leads to the second aspect of the work of messenger / apostles, they will gather new converts into churches where they can be discipled, nurtured and fed. In the New Testament new churches were planted by the 'apostolic team', not by the sending church or churches. Antioch did not plant the churches in Derbe, Iconium and Lystra, Paul and Barnabas did, and neither would it seem did Antioch have any ongoing role, responsibility or authority over the new churches. They were the responsibility of the team.

Where the new church was concerned the first priority was the establishing of the right foundations. Each church was to be ***'built on the foundation of the apostles and prophets, with Christ Jesus himself as the chief cornerstone' [Ephesians 2:20]***. In one sense these foundations were those of the 'Apostles of the Lamb' : ***'the apostles' teaching' [Acts 2:42]***, the faith ***'once for all entrusted to the saints' [Jude 1:3]***. In another sense they were to be laid practically in the life of a new church by an 'architect', the meaning of Paul's phrase 'expert builder' [ἀρχιτέκτων], who contributes knowledge not labour, supervising how others built on his foundation : ***'By the grace God has given me, I laid a foundation as an expert builder, and someone else is building on it. But each one should be careful how he builds [1 Corinthians 3:10]***. They laid a foundation for others, elders, pastors and teachers to build on. Paul and his team did not try to put the roof on the house. Herbert Harrison highlights the importance of recognizing how different gifts function : *'An uncoordinated bunch of plumbers, bricklayers, and carpenters, no matter how skilled, will never build the church. Wise master builders are the key.'*[53]

Such a distinguishing between particular gifts is not a matter of status, but of role in service. The fact that ***'God has appointed first of all apostles' [1 Corinthians 12:28]*** is an order of function not superiority. Apostles were the initial 'foundation layers' : 'This was an apostolic task. *He was now writing to a pagan church far away from Jerusalem, years after the day of Pentecost, and reflecting on what he did at Corinth, he said, 'I laid a foundation.' That was a dynamic act performed in a local church that he could quantify, not just a philosophical concept for the universal church. It resulted in a church being properly founded. Notice that Paul laid a foundation long after the original foundation had been laid in Jerusalem.'*[54]

This was why Barnabas was sent by the apostles in Jerusalem to set things

53 Herbert Harrison in 'Redemption' magazine 1986

54 Terry Virgo in Newfrontiers Magazine Volume 2 - Issue 04 - September-November 2003 page 10

in order in Antioch. He brought in Paul to help the process, *'Barnabas went to Tarsus to look for Saul, and when he found him, he brought him to Antioch. So for a whole year Barnabas and Saul met with the church and taught great numbers of people' [Acts 11:25-6].* Both Barnabas and Paul who did this work are described as apostles. Perhaps Agabus was sent for the same purpose, to give the prophetic foundation : *'During this time some prophets came down from Jerusalem to Antioch. One of them, named Agabus, stood up and through the Spirit predicted that a severe famine would spread over the entire Roman world' [Acts 11:27-9].* There was no intention of leaving the converts in Antioch 'to get on with it' without the necessary gifts. Presumably, Peter and John went to Samaria for the same purpose, *'when the apostles in Jerusalem heard that Samaria had accepted the word of God, they sent Peter and John to them' [Acts 8:14].* *'When the apostles at Jerusalem heard that Samaria had received the word of God, they did not regard it simply as an evangelistic breakthrough; they recognized their own authority and responsibility to put in right foundations and build a dynamic community.'* [55]

The apostolic gift is the catalyst that enables what has been rightly taught to be implemented.

The apostolic gift is the catalyst that enables what has been rightly taught to be implemented. The truths would be taught and then applied to the context, with the team facilitating the process of implementation. Only then could it be said that the necessary foundations had been laid. It involves doctrinal clarity, but also the structures and recognition of gifts that can see the outworking of truth implemented in healthy church life. The team was responsible for 'setting out' and 'digging' the foundations on which others would build the superstructure. Straying from these foundations in later building would lead to instability and decay.

It is interesting to see how comfortable Paul was for others to build on his foundations. Even though he had planted the church in Corinth he encouraged Apollos, who had a teaching ministry, to follow him there and to consolidate the work : *'When Apollos wanted to go to Achaia, the brothers encouraged him and wrote to the disciples there to welcome him. On arriving, he was a great help to those who by grace had believed. For he vigorously refuted the Jews in public debate, proving from the Scriptures that Jesus was*

55 Terry Virgo Op.cit page 9

the Christ. While Apollos was at Corinth, Paul took the road through the interior and arrived at Ephesus' [Acts 18:24-91:1]. As he explained to Corinth, *'I planted the seed, Apollos watered it, but God made it grow' [1 Corinthians 3:6].*

The importance of this role in planting new churches, or in transitioning struggling churches, is at the heart of healthy church life. It involves extensive teaching of Biblical truth, applying it in the given situation, and helping the leaders responsible to see the process through. Paul's repeated visits to Corinth and at least three letters were for this very purpose. He, and his team, were aware of the practical and spiritual needs of the churches, and would respond as appropriate by visiting, writing or sending a team member. *'The foundation-layers were also foundation-repairers. If the spiritual welfare of a congregation was seriously threatened - that is, if its foundations were shaken or endangered through backsliding, strife, false doctrine or the unfaithfulness of its Elders - to the extent that the Head of the Church could no longer speak to it directly, He would do so through His foundation-layers.'*[56] The ministry of the apostolic team was vital to the on-going health of the individual churches.

Paul said that `the care of all the churches' weighed heavily upon him. His ministry kept the churches sound and faithful, *'preventing the Corinthians from becoming engulfed in sin and disorder, the Galatians from falling hopelessly into error and Diotrephes from continuing to usurp authority'.*[57]

Defending truth against error is still needed. Having 'messengers' who come from outside, with an objectivity to see what is being taught that is not caught up in the latest fad or sucked into error by degrees, is a security for any local church. Teaching grace and exposing legalism is a much neglected apostolic ministry. Despite the foundations laid in Antioch it was necessary for 'messengers' from Jerusalem to visit to clarify truth in the church, and then move on to others. *'Then the apostles and elders, with the whole church, decided to choose some of their own men and send them to Antioch with Paul and Barnabas. They chose Judas (called Barsabbas) and Silas, two men who were leaders among the brothers [Acts 15:22].* The 'messengers' were to bring and apply the truths of the Gospel to the churches. They were to take the truths of Scripture and pass them on like a baton. *'And the things you have heard me say in the presence of many witnesses entrust to reliable men who will also be qualified to teach others' [2 Timothy 2:2]. 'They were there to carry*

56 Alex R. Hay Op.cit page 124

57 Alex R. Hay Op.cit page 232

out the directions that Paul gave by continuing and/or completing the unfinished work. Similarly Paul expected Timothy to maintain or continue His own ministry. He was not at liberty to develop his own message, the received message had to be passed on.

Not only did Timothy have to personally pass it on, but also he had to ensure that his hearers also passed it on.'[58] Teachers could teach the same truths but not with the same authority and insight into what was actually needed in a particular church's foundations. It is a matter of gift, and apostles were 'master builders' with these needed gifts.

Once the church had been 'founded', however, the team moved on. Sometimes this was by force of circumstances, as in Thessalonica, elsewhere it was when the job was fully done, as in Corinth, where it was after two years [Acts 19:10]. Paul was always eager to press on to new fields, leaving the new church to stand on their own feet after the initial foundations had been laid. Frank Viola suggests an average of three to five months spent with a church in the initial period.[59] Paul stayed long enough to give adequate teaching and lay a solid foundation, and if he was forced to leave prematurely, e.g. from Thessalonica, he made sure the process was completed by team members or by letter.

Apostles never stayed to become pastors.

He did not allow them to become dependent on him in a wrong way, as a permanently resident pastor or teacher. In a comparatively short time he left them, encouraging them to take full responsibility for their growth and order. They had still much to learn and much experience to gain, but he had provided them with a sufficient basis upon which to begin their work. Apostles never stayed to become pastors, or took the role for the security the local situation could bring. One of the greatest dangers would have been to encourage paternalism, treating the converts as children and not as adults. It would be all too easy for leaders who have the care of a daughter church to take a paternalistic attitude to meet their own emotional needs, being the central figure and controlling every detail of a congregation's activities.

Titus was given a job on Crete, ***'the reason I left you in Crete was that you might straighten out what was left unfinished and appoint elders in every***

58 Bernard Lewis Op.cit

59 Frank Viola Op.cit page 79

town, as I directed you' [Titus 1:5], but was then to move on, *'as soon as I send Artemas or Tychicus to you, do your best to come to me at Nicopolis' [Titus 3:12]*. Titus is also known to have been in Corinth [2 Corinthians 7:6], Jerusalem [Galatians 2:1], and Dalmatia [2 Timothy 4:10]. Paul sent Timothy to Corinth and made arrangements for his onward journey, but never to stay : *'If Timothy comes, see to it that he has nothing to fear while he is with you, for he is carrying on the work of the Lord, just as I am. No one, then, should refuse to accept him. Send him on his way in peace so that he may return to me. I am expecting him along with the brothers' [1 Corinthians 16:10]*. Roland Allen put the issues succinctly, *'to leave new-born churches to learn by experience is apostolic, to abandon them is not apostolic: to watch over them is apostolic, to be always nursing them is not apostolic: to guide their education is apostolic, to provide it for them is not apostolic.*[60]

The third phase in the work of the apostles / messengers was to be a link to the wider mission for the churches they had founded or helped to establish. Though the team may have moved on 'messengers' were sent back to re-visit as needs arose, or simply to maintain the contact. Team members travelled long distances to carry letters or simply to take and bring news: *'Tychicus, the dear brother and faithful servant in the Lord, will tell you everything, so that you also may know how I am and what I am doing. I am sending him to you for this very purpose, that you may know how we are, and that he may encourage you' [Ephesians 6:21 & 22], 'I am sending him to you for the express purpose that you may know about our circumstances and that he may encourage your hearts. He is coming with Onesimus, our faithful and dear brother, who is one of you. They will tell you everything that is happening here' [Colossians 4:8]*. Building and keeping the links with the churches was very important. No doubt there would be regional contact between churches where geography permitted it, such as between Ephesus and Colossae, but the principal links for a church were with the team. Such links prevented isolation, independency, discouragement, and lack of accountability. To have the team members visiting would re-kindle vision, prayer, zeal and commitment for the ongoing mission to regions and nations.

As a result there was a real sense of togetherness. The churches were linked by visits, prayer and giving. The Ephesians could be called to *'keep on praying for all the saints' [Ephesians 6:18]*, not just for those in their own congregation or for the churches in their own locality. Equally, Paul could

60 Roland Allen 'The Spontaneous Expansion of the Church' page 150

exhort the Gentile churches to give financial help to their fellow-believers who were enduring poverty in Judea [Acts 11:25-30] without apology or awkwardness. Many of the journeys of the 'messengers' were in part related to the gathering or distribution of funds.

The churches were autonomous, led by elders, without a federal organization, headquarters, presiding council or hierarchy. They benefited from a relational structure, based on trust, in which apostles had earned the right to send, command and instruct. Alec Motyer describing the relationship between the churches says, *'the impression we receive of the New Testament is of local churches loosely federated under apostolic authority, with each church managing its own affairs under the leadership of overseers and deacons.'*[61] The churches were neither dependent on the team, nor independent of it. The relationships built in founding the church, or through on-going personal contact with a church founded by others [e.g. Rome], meant an on-going care and willingness to give and receive help. There was no attempt to control, dictate or call for blind obedience.

Sadly, as noted earlier, authority in the churches was soon centralised through the development of church 'councils' from the middle of the second century. Regional leaders would gather to make decisions for all the churches. Some have pointed to Acts 15, the so called 'Council of Jerusalem', as being the first of these, but that gathering was in response to Antioch's struggles with the legalists. It was not a gathering of regional leaders but merely, ***'the apostles and elders'*** *[Acts 15:3]* of the Jerusalem church. Similarly, when Paul went to Jerusalem he saw ***'Peter and stayed with him fifteen days. [He] saw none of the other apostles—only James, the Lord's brother'*** *[Galatians 1:18]*. There was no over-arching hierarchy or central authority in the first century. The later change, however, had a dramatic effect. The ministry of apostles / messengers, who exercised a spiritual ministry with only spiritual authority, was replaced by that of the Diocesan Bishop as the power of local leaders grew. Bishops, with regional authority and ever increasing ecclesiastical power, replaced the 'messengers'. Cyprian claimed that the bishops were the successors to the apostles but in fact ecclesiastical authority was substituted for spiritual authority. *'It was an irreparable loss. No longer were there foundation layers and repairers for the extension of the Church and to minister to congregations that fell into difficulties.*[62]

61 Alec Motyer 'The Message of Philippians', quoted by Terry Virgo in Newfrontiers Magazine Volume 2 - Issue 04 - September-November 2003 page 6

62 Alex R. Hay Op.cit page 251

This change from relational networks to institutional control moved the emphasis from extension to maintenance. Churches were getting decisions not visits as authority moved from local elders to higher officials. The centrality of the Gospel, and the evangelism and church planting that came from it, was gradually lost. The effects were to linger through the centuries of Christendom so that patterns and attitudes became assumed as normal and original, when they were not. The effects are still with us, hence the need for a thorough re-examination of our real roots. Titles are not the important thing. *'What matters is that the purpose for which the apostle exists is actually attained - however it is going to be done. It is not important that we have men called apostles, but that we have people doing the work of 'apostleing'.'*[63]

63 Roger Forster, quoted in William K Kay 'Apostolic Networks in Britain' page 115

Chapter Five : The Make-up of the Teams

Paul was a team man. People were attracted to work with him, and there were many who did. It is difficult with some of the names he mentions in his letters to know whether they were former or current team members, or members of churches he had visited. The long list in Romans 16 is all the more remarkable because at that time he had never been to Rome. He certainly had a good memory for names! *'Paul attracted friends around him as a magnet attracts iron filings.'* [64]

The list of names in the New Testament is an impressive one when they are brought together :

Agabus	Epaphras	Luke	Sosthenes
Apollos	Epaphroditus	Onesimus	Stephanas
Aristarchus	Erastus	Onesiphorus	Timothy
Artemas	Gaius	Priscilla & Aquila	Titus
Barnabas	Jesus [Justus]	Secundus	Trophimus
Clement	John Mark	Silas	Tychicus
Crecens	Lucas	Sopater	Zenas
Demas	Lucius	Sosipater	

He seemed to gather new members for the team at regular intervals as he travelled, at times almost one from each church he planted. The list of names in Acts 20:4 represent a time-line of his journey : ***'He was accompanied by Sopater son of Pyrrhus from Berea, Aristarchus and Secundus from Thessalonica, Gaius from Derbe, Timothy also, and Tychicus and Trophimus from the province of Asia'*** *[Acts 20:4]*. They started in their native region and then travelled into foreign provinces. Alex Hay suggests, with some justification, that Paul tended to keep them on the team when they were in their native areas before they were replaced by others when the team moved into another culture. *'On the so-called second and third journeys, Paul, after ministering again in his own native Cilicia, went gradually further a-field, to Greece and Macedonia, and later to the other Provinces of Asia Minor, but, as he did so, we find men from these regions being joined to the company: Timothy, from Lycaonia, Titus a Greek, Tychicus and Trophimus from Asia,*

64 F F Bruce 'The Pauline Circle' page 8, quoted in Barney Coombs 'Apostles Today' page 41

Aristarchus from Macedonia, etc. Also, it will be noted that when members of the company were sent to visit different churches, those chosen were often men who came from the region to be visited." [65] Some team members such as Timothy, Silas and Luke are exceptions, and it is likely that some stepped out from the team for reasons other than geography.

Potential was to be gathered, envisioned and developed at every opportunity.

However, it was an ever-revolving door, and few had any sense of permanence. They came from churches, or even his own family, and so had a track record or recommendation, and there does not seem to be a quota he was trying to fill. He picked up future leaders continuously. Potential was to be gathered, envisioned and developed at every opportunity. Some have suggested that they were initially sent by the churches with funds and then stayed. Sadly, as will always be the case, some left for the wrong reasons. *'Demas send greetings' [Colossians 4:14]*, after a few years becomes *'Demas, because he loved this world, has deserted me and has gone to Thessalonica' [2 Timothy 4:10].*

What is clear, apart from uncomfortable exceptions, is that Paul rarely travelled or worked alone. The team gave mutual fellowship, encouragement, protection and training as well as a variety of gifts and a visible model of plurality in leadership. *'This methodology involves a church planting team or an apostolic band. The team functions as a church even as a church grows up around it, providing a context for discipleship and a demonstration of Christian community.'* [66]

After travelling with Paul for a while the team members would also stay behind after Paul moved on, or go on ahead of him, or go on without him on a revisit or to a new area. Timothy joined Paul and Silas at Lystra *[Acts 16:1]*, stayed behind at Berea and Thessalonica when Paul was chased out *[Acts 17:14, 1 Thessalonians 3:2]*, joined Paul at Corinth *[Acts 18:5, 2 Corinthians 1:19]*, and was sent to Macedonia without Paul *[Acts 19:22, 1 Corinthians 4:17, 16:10]*. He subsequently journeyed to Philippi *[Philippians 2:19]*, joined Paul and then went to Troas *[Acts 20:4]* and Ephesus *[1 Timothy 1:3]*, before joining Paul at Rome and in prison *[2 Timothy 4:9, Hebrews 13:23]*. Whether with Paul, or working separately, they acted as 'co-workers'

65 Alex R Hay Op.cit page 82

66 Tim Chester and Steve Timmis 'Total Church' IVP 2007 page 89

doing the same work in the same way. Paul could say of Timothy that, *'he is carrying on the work of the Lord, just as I am' [1 Corinthians 16:10]*, and often conveyed Paul's message *[1 Corinthians 4:16]*. Titus had *'the same concern I have for you' [2 Corinthians 8:16]* acting *'in the same spirit and follow[ing] the same course' [2 Corinthians 12 :18]* willingly, *'for Titus not only welcomed our appeal, but he is coming to you with much enthusiasm and on his own initiative' [2 Corinthians 8:17]*. *'Paul does not call his fellow-workers `Apostolic Delegates'. He calls Titus `a partner with me', `my comrade in my labours' and refers to others of his brethren as `apostles' (2 Cor. 8:23). He speaks of Epaphroditus as `my brother and comrade' and an 'apostle'.'* [67] Several of his letters are sent from members of the team, suggesting co-authorship *[2 Corinthians, Philippians, Philemon and Colossians, 1 & 2 Thessalonians]*. This was not 'top-down' leadership.

Some members seemed to work more closely with the team than others. Titus is often mentioned working out from the team, but his name does not appear in Acts which follows Paul's movements. Apollos's path often crosses Paul's but only rarely do they seem to travel together. This would be natural if he followed Paul, as at Corinth, watering what Paul had sown. He was certainly free to follow his own course and schedule. *'Now about our brother Apollos: I strongly urged him to go to you with the brothers. He was quite unwilling to go now, but he will go when he has the opportunity' [1 Corinthians 16:12]*. If Apollos was a teacher linked to the team, then Silas was a prophet, *'Judas and Silas, who themselves were prophets, said much to encourage and strengthen the brothers' [Acts 15:32]*. Andronicus and Junias were apostles / messengers *[Romans 16:7]*. There was a varied 'gift-mix' in the team.

Some of those to whom Paul gave the title 'messenger' [ἀποστολος] were also part of the team but seem to have had a link to a particular church for a season, on behalf of the team. Timothy had spent extended time in Corinth and Ephesus, and Titus in Corinth, Crete and Dalmatia. Epaphras is linked to Colossae *[Colossians 1:7, 4:12&13]* and Epaphroditus is mentioned as having a strong link with Philippi. *'But I think it is necessary to send back to you Epaphroditus, my brother, fellow worker and fellow soldier, who is also your messenger [ἀποστολος], whom you sent to take care of my needs. For he longs for all of you and is distressed because you heard he was ill. ...Welcome him in the Lord with great joy, and honour men like him' [Philippians 2:25]*.

67 Alex R. Hay Op.cit page 99

In this ministry these 'New Testament Teams' preached and taught the Gospel, modelled the dynamics of the kingdom of God, and laid foundations for a healthy church. They equipped and matured the saints *[Ephesians 4:12&13]*, appointed local leadership *[Acts 14:23]*, brought clarity and impartiality in serious cases of church discipline *[1 Corinthians 5:4&5]* and kept the church looking outward to its mission to their region and the nations.

The Early Church had an itinerant ministry to serve the Gospel and the churches as well as local ministry. These teams, and the ministry they performed to new and struggling churches, were a key ingredient of the apostolic mission and no doubt a factor in its effectiveness. We should seek to do things in a New Testament way and not pass over patterns of ministry that are clearly retained in Scripture for our instruction and benefit.

Chapter Six : A New Testament Model

Most New Testament letters were addressed to particular churches, but three were addressed to actual team members sent out by Paul to finish work he had begun in local churches. Paul wrote two letters to Timothy and one to Titus as *'ministers on the move',* helping Titus to lay foundations in Crete and Timothy to strengthen believers in Ephesus. The issues raised in the letters, therefore, give an insight into what was involved in laying foundations in a local church. A study of Paul's letter to Titus, with further illustrations from those to Timothy, will serve as a helpful model to show how things worked, and the kind of work that was done by the team.

Titus is not mentioned as part of Paul's teams in the Acts of the Apostles but in his letters he is clearly working with Paul and others in the apostolic work in Corinth, Jerusalem, Crete and Dalmatia. In Paul's letter to Titus he addresses him as *'my true child' [Titus 1:4]* and elsewhere as *'my partner and fellow worker' [2 Cor.8:23]*. He works alongside Paul *'on his own initiative' [2 Cor. 8:17]*, from 'the same concern' [2 Cor. 8:16], and in the *'same spirit, following the same course' [2 Cor.8:23]*. He is described specifically as one of the *'representatives of the churches [ἀπόστολοι ἐκκλησιῶν] and an honour to Christ' [2 Cor.8:23]*.

Titus was left in Crete to *'straighten out what was left unfinished and appoint elders in every town' [Titus 1:5]*. He was to straighten what was crooked and complete what was unfinished.[68] The work that Paul had begun in laying doctrinal, behavioural, leadership and functional foundations was to be completed by the team members in his absence, and where things had begun to develop wrongly they were to 'reset' the foundations.

The work that Paul had begun in laying doctrinal, behavioural, leadership and functional foundations was to be completed by the team members in his absence.

Paul begins the letter with a description of the remit for the work the team was doing : *'an apostle of Jesus Christ for the faith of God's elect and the knowledge of the truth that leads to godliness ... through the preaching entrusted to me by the command of God our Saviour' [Titus 1:1-3]*. They were

68 John Stott 'The Message of 1 Timothy and Titus' page 173

to nurture the faith of God's elect, to confirm them in the truth, and shape them in godliness, building on the work of preaching that brought them to Christ in the first place.

The letter gives practical instructions for the setting of these foundations, and 'charges' to the team members and the church :

1. The first 'foundational' aspect concerned the second part of Titus' mandate to ***'straighten out what was left unfinished and appoint elders in every town, as I directed you'*** *[Titus 1:4]*. Paul first of all lays leadership foundations for the future. He gives careful criteria for those being considered as elders to lead the emerging church *[Titus 1:6-9]*. He does the same for Timothy, with further instructions concerning deacons *[1 Tim. 3:1-13, 5:17-24]*. Paul is giving directions on the needed character, track-record and reputation of leaders, as well as the authority to appoint them. Elders were to be appointed by the team, not elected by the church, though the qualities set out in these letters would require a full consultation with the church.
2. The second aspect was to lay and confirm clear doctrinal foundations. Paul would have done much of this already before leaving Crete, but the coming of Jewish teachers meant that the basic truths of the Gospel had to be defined and defended once again. Titus was to teach against ***'rebellious people, mere talkers and deceivers, especially those of the circumcision group.'*** *[Titus 1:10]* ***'... Jewish myths or ... the commands of those who reject the truth'*** *[Titus 1:14]* ***'... foolish controversies and genealogies and arguments and quarrels about the law, because these are unprofitable and useless'*** *[Titus 3:9]*. He wrote similarly to Timothy *[1 Tim.1:3-7, 20, 4:1-10, 2 Tim. 2:8-13]*, clarifying the right and wrong use of the Law *[1 Tim.1:8,9]*. The truth was to be taught, kept clear, and defended. It was grounded in the Scriptures *[2 Tim.3:10-17]* which were to be followed, expounded, applied and learned. There was to be no compromise or concession at all with false teachers. These were the things for Titus to teach, encourage and rebuke ***'with all authority.'*** *[Titus 2:15]*. The team was also to train others in the church to ensure an ongoing clarity *[2 Tim. 2:2]*.
3. The third aspect of 'foundation laying' was to set patterns for behaviour, relationships and attitudes. God's truth had logical and inevitable consequences for lifestyle. Titus was to ***'teach what is in accord with***

sound doctrine' [Titus 2:1]. Timothy was to *'teach and urge' [1 Tim. 6:2]*. The grace of God *[Titus 2:11, 3:4-7]* was to rule out certain behaviour, attitudes and impurity *[Titus 2:12-14]*. New Christians had to be taught how to behave in a new Christian community that was being built. This included instructions on :

a. Relationships and attitudes in church and family *[Titus 2:2-10, 1 Tim. 2:9-15, 5:1-16]*.

b. Behaviour in society *[Titus 3:1-3, 8, 1 Tim. 6:1,2]*.

c. Handling problem people *[Titus 3:9-11, 2 Tim. 3:1-9]*.

d. The church's praying *[1 Tim. 2:1-8]*.

Paul also gives clear instruction to his team about how they are to conduct themselves and fulfil their ministry. He told Titus who were to be silenced *[Titus 1:11]*, rebuked *[Titus 1:13]* and urged on *[Titus 2:6]*. Titus does seem to work with a large degree of autonomy under Paul's overall direction, whereas Timothy gets much fuller encouragement and exhortation. Much of the first letter and most of the second letter is personal encouragement, testimony and solemn charges to Timothy for him to implement. *[1 Tim. 1:18,19, 4:11-16, 6:6-16, 20, 2 Tim. 2:1-7, 14-26, 4:1-5]*. The team was to be clear in terms of their role and responsibilities.

The letters usually closed with news of the wider team, plans and issues that members needed to be aware of *[Titus 3:12-15, 2 Tim. 1:15-18, 4:6-8, 19-22]*. They were to care for and help each other as well as the churches they were serving. Though for a period they were in different places, they were a team. Paul made sure that they did not settle or overstay their time in a particular church, but arranged for Artemas or Tychicus to replace Titus so he could return to Paul and the ongoing mission *[Titus 3:12,13]*.

At first sight it might be asked why it was necessary for team members to travel to lay, or re-lay, such foundations. Could not the emerging leaders in the church lay their own foundations : appoint their own leaders, define their own doctrine from the Scriptures, and set the expectations for individuals, families and church? Clearly not.

- Experience and gift were essential to recognizing the right elders and how they were to lead. Democracy and secular models of leadership and management were not deemed adequate to Paul. Personal agendas and favouritism could so easily lead to the wrong people being in leadership. Objective external wisdom was essential.

- Truth was not a matter of personal interpretation! Sound doctrines, and particularly their defence against current heresies needed to be squarely grounded on 'apostolic doctrine', based on the 'God breathed' Scriptures. For Paul this was not an early form of institutional hierarchy where doctrines are decided in an incipient Vatican, but a question of gift and insight of how truth hangs together. In the busyness of local church it was not always easy to spot developing error, especially if the people spreading it were 'nice' and respected. Objectivity and a measure of detachment from the situation were essential.
- Life, family and church had to be built. Wise counsel helped with each, and no-one got it right without insightful counsel. How to 'do church' was not merely the result of tradition, pragmatics and strong personalities, but of God-given gift and experience. A house needs an architect, a 'wise master builder'. Some had a special gift for helping churches grow healthily. Evangelists, pastors and teachers had essential gifts in the dynamic growth of the Early Church, but the ability to see clearly what was needed at a particular phase of a church's development, and to deliver it, was what apostolic team did best.

Paul's letters show the principles at work in Crete and Ephesus. That such ministry and input were necessary then is noteworthy. The lack of them in contemporary church plants, and struggling churches, might explain in part the evident lack of progress, growth and even survival.

Chapter Seven : Historical Parallels - Welsh Methodism

It can be justifiably argued that the revivals of the eighteenth century were the closest that Britain has ever come to an 'apostolic era'. Not only was the threat of political revolution averted, but a spiritual revolution took place across the length and breadth of the land that laid the foundation for the massive growth of Nonconformity in the next century.

The revivals of the eighteenth century were the closest that Britain has ever come to an "apostolic era".

In England this was spread largely through the Wesley brothers and those who worked with them. From a small and cautious beginning the Gospel came to be heard on commons, roads and town squares by hundreds and thousands of people. Societies of believers were formed in most towns and even villages across the counties and hundreds of exhorters, a new brand of itinerant preacher, were trained, commissioned and organised for the task, despite relentless persecution. At the same time in parts of England, Scotland and particularly North America George Whitefield and his associates were developing a parallel work.

The process in Wales began slightly earlier led by a group of leaders in their twenties, notably Howell Harries, Daniel Rowland and William Williams. They too had profound experiences of conversion, experienced remarkable empowerment of the Holy Spirit, especially in preaching, and began to travel to widen and sustain a growing national movement.

Howell Harris was the first to begin to travel to support his 'societies'. It all began when a Mrs Parry, Talyllyn, invited him to come to her house to instruct her friends and neighbours. This was followed by other invitations and as people were converted others joined him as 'exhorters', travelling to evangelise and instruct the infant societies. Harris was converted in 1735 and by June 15th 1741 he could write that *'Thomas James of Builth, ...looking after the Societies above Builth; Benjamin Cadman in Montgomeryshire; Joseph about Trevecka and below Brecon; John Powell above Brecon till Neath; John Williams, Llwynyberllan, about Llanddovery; Jack of Errwd about Llandevalle, &c., and to overlook all; Richard Jones about Carmarthen;*

69 D E Jenkins 'Calvinistic Methodist Holy Orders' : Carnarvon 1911 page 31

besides brethren and others going about elsewhere in Monmouth, Glamorgan, and Pembroke and Cardigan shires.[69] It is remarkable that he had 'itinerants' operating across South Wales so quickly. It was the key to the effectiveness of what followed.

Because of growing opposition from church authorities the leaders decided to meet to set the movement on a more organized footing. They met at Dugoedydd, a house north of Llandovery, in January, 1742, and later nearby at Llwyn-y-berllan in February. George Whitefield had recommended a monthly meeting of leaders to identify who should be recognized as preachers / exhorters for local, regional or wider spheres, and so they could report back on their efforts. *'If you had monthly meetings, each exhorter or labourer might communicate his success; an abstract might be sent over to England; and we in return would send you an abstract of our affairs. Unity would thereby be promoted, love increased, and our hands strengthened, and we should be like an army with banners.'*[70] They discussed *'What to do for God and how to promote His glory'* and agreed who should go where and who was responsible for which areas. There were four Anglican ministers present and eighteen exhorters, six of them full-time. Most were in their twenties, acknowledging *'we are a heap of boys, o pity us!'*[71] They published 'Rules of the Societies' to give some consistency and agreed on doctrinal and practical matters to ensure right foundations. Howell Harris, as early as 1739, had seen his role as to *'go about the societies, to root and establish them in God's truth.'*[72] In August, 1740, he was *'settling four societies and putting them in Christian discipline'*[73] By July 1742 *'I did look over the poor dear lambs, and I found there was in Breconshire about 15 Societies, and in Glamorganshire about 15, in Carmarthenshire about 10 or 12, and in Monmouthshire about the same; and between Hereford, Radnor, and Montgomery shires about 15; and in Pembrokeshire and Cardiganshire ...a good number".*[74]

70 Eifion Evans 'Daniel Rowland' : Banner of Truth Trust, Edinburgh 1985 page 177

71 D E Jenkins Op.cit page 59

72 Eifion Evans 'Daniel Rowland' page 82

73 Eifion Evans 'Daniel Rowland' page 106

74 D E Jenkins Op.cit page 76

In January 1743 the leaders again met, this time led by George Whitefield, and full minutes were kept of who was to do what, and where, as they *'settled public and private exhorters.'*[75] The ministers had a wider brief with Howell Harries acting as a *'Superintendent over Wales.'*

The exhorters came from all across South Wales :

Richard Tibbott to be the General Visitor of the Bands.
James Williams to visit the Societies at Cayo, Talley, Llanfynydd & Llangathen
Morgan Hughes: Cayo, Lledrod, Rhydfendigaid
David Williams: Lledrod, Llanilar
Rice Thomas: Pont ar Gamddwr, Caron
John Powell: Defynnog
William Evans: Llanddewi, Llandecle, Llandrindod
Howell Griffith: Llantrissant, Glynogwr
Richard Thomas: Llanedern, and to assist at Waterford
Evan Thomas: Mynyddislwyn
Thos Price to the Care of Waterford
Stephen Jones: Glasgoed, Goetre
Tho' Lewis: Pentyrch, New house
Richard Jones and John Deer: Byrthin, Llanilltyd, Aberthaw
Charles Powell: Glasbury, Bronllys
John Jones: Cwmdy, Grwynefechan
Morgan John: Palleg, Creinant, Llanddeusant, Cwmamman

William Williams was given, *'the general care of these exhorters and societies' and later was, 'to leave his curacies and be an assistant to the Rev Mr Rowlands.'*[76] In this he began a travelling ministry of immense influence.

These 'Associations' followed regularly to order a growing and widening work. Teams of exhorters worked in areas under the oversight of an overall ordained clergyman. Williams looked after Ceredigion and Carmarthenshire, Howell Davies over Pembrokeshire, Harris over the South and eventually North Wales. The work of the itinerants spearheaded a movement that in two generations had spread to most communities in Wales.

Interestingly, in the nineteenth century the 'exhorters' became local church elders and the ministers, who had been itinerant preachers and overseers, became settled pastors. Needless to say the momentum was lost.

75 D.E.Jenkins Op.cit page 90

76 'Early Association Records' in 'Cylchgrawn Cymdeithas Hanes Eglwys Methodistiaeth Calfinaidd Cymru' Vol. XLVIII No.2 page 39

Chapter Eight : Lessons for Today - 2

The issue that should be faced at this point is whether the patterns of ministry, both local and itinerant, are clearly in the New Testament narrative, and whether that has any bearing for today. With the serious decline of the major denominations over recent decades and the evident failure of the liberal theology and nominalism that were so common in them, the tendency has been to reject all forms of networks or associations of churches, preferring the 'safety' of some form of 'independency'.

If churches are not independent in name, ...they tend to be in practice.

Independent churches with no formal link to other churches, and more importantly, no regular ministry from outside, have become normal in evangelical and charismatic / evangelical circles. If churches are not 'independent' in name because of historic connections, they tend to be in practice. The effect of this has been the loss of a sense of mission to the region, let alone the nation. Churches tend to be preoccupied with their own needs and locality only, with some investment in overseas mission or emergency relief through missionary societies or smaller initiatives.

Whether such a pattern can be defended from Scripture is doubtful. It is the product of painful history and the individualism of contemporary culture, not careful exegesis of the New Testament. According to the Evangelical Movement of Wales, *'the New Testament knows nothing at all of the isolation into which the independency principle has sometimes degenerated.'* [77]

The issues could be ignored if it were not for the fact that towns and villages are increasingly devoid of vibrant Christian churches, and where there are struggling churches or new church plants their prospects are not encouraging. Howell Harries looked at the situation in his day, where the few independent churches had largely drawn back into defensive mode, and concluded, that independency was *'not right.'* [78] Instead, he and those with him fostered teams to serve the groups committed to their vision and ministry. In the early days of Welsh and English Methodism this did not involve new denominations, institutions or legal structures, and it does not need to now.

77 'The Christian Church - a Biblical study' Op.cit page 17

78 D E Jenkins Op.cit page 145

Instead, the building of strong, trusting relationships of loyalty, cooperation and shared vision is needed urgently. The concept of 'Churches Together on a Mission', individual churches setting sail together like ships in an armada [without ropes tying them together!], has much to commend it.[79]

At a time with similar challenges John Calvin in his commentary on Isaiah 49:21 said, *'The Lord, who has no need of human aid, begets his children in an extraordinary manner, and by the astonishing power of his Spirit; and 'brings them up' wherever he thinks proper; and in the fulfilment of this prediction, the Lord supplied them with nurses contrary to the expectation of all, so that it is not without reason that the Church wonders how they were reared. When we read this prophecy we are reminded that we ought not to be distressed beyond measure, if at any time we see the Church resemble a 'bereaved' woman, and that we ought not to doubt that he can suddenly, or in a moment, raise up and restore her, though we perceive no means by which she can be restored'.*[80] *The practical outworking of this was impressive, 'When Calvin heard of an isolated Christian or even of an isolated group trying to gather by themselves, he was there on the doorstep, as it were, with a messenger and a letter, seeking to make them feel they were part of a far larger group in touch with the universal church which was praying for them, and had a word for them, and was seeking to support them in every practical way. Each small group that appeared, he regarded as the nucleus of a congregation which must be made to grow and define itself to receive as a pastor one of the numbers he had trained for the purpose of such leadership under the Word of God. ... Within each congregation he sought to develop a cellular structure in which under wise and trained leadership each individual would give the other support, enlightenment and encouragement.'*[81]

The challenges arising, therefore, are straightforward yet fundamental to the process of doing church effectively :

- The need for the ministry of 'New Testament Teams' into all churches should be acknowledged. For mature churches it will be merely a relationship of fellowship, envisioning and counsel, with the safeguard in place for when future crises arise. For new or transitioning churches it would be a life-line that would prevent prolonged years of unnecessary struggle and loneliness, or even closure.

79 Concepts of 'Newfrontiers' www.newfrontiers.xtn.org

80 Calvin's Commentaries Baker 1989

81 Ronald S Wallace, Calvin, Geneva and the Reformation' p. 158

- This acknowledgement should lead to an adoption of the principles in practice. Links should be made, relationships built and objectives agreed. Churches and leaders would begin to identify those with the gifts to be part of such a team, *'speak well of them' [Acts 16:2]*, and look for ways to release them to such a ministry. This may or may not involve financial investment, but it will involve prayer, counsel, planning and accountability support.
- We should recognize that not all churches are built on good foundations. Bad foundations may be doctrinal [or due to the lack of any doctrinal clarity at all], relational [personality splits rarely lead to harmonious churches], visionary [inward looking, not Gospel centred], functional [irrelevant practices, fads and distractions] etc.. Inviting people with the right gifts is not an admission of failure, incompetence or weakness, but evidence of wisdom, humility and acknowledgement that gifts are given, *'according to the grace given us' [Romans 12:6]*. Pride, ego, and insecurity in leaders will never build strong churches. Loyalty, meekness, and submission to godly leadership will.
- When team members are welcomed a relationship of trust should be given time to grow. It may be necessary to challenge favourite elements and traditions that confine and inhibit. A 'safe pace' is helpful. Equally, the team should be allowed to work with church and leaders to see the suggested remedies implemented, and not just the giving of advice. The team will need to spend weeks, months or years with the church to see the process through.
- Churches that have developed their own traditions and comfort zones should be re-orientated to being 'Gospel driven'. Maintaining an outward looking focus in the life of a local church, that can be all too easily preoccupied with crises and pastoral issues, needs the regular input and envisioning of people with apostolic and evangelistic gifts.
- If the gifts from the ascended Christ of, *'some to be apostles, some to be prophets, some to be evangelists, and some to be pastors and teachers' [Ephesians 4:11]*, are accepted in terms of function, if not title, then churches should ask themselves where they are going to find and draw on foundational, directional, outreaching, caring and instructional ministry. These 'gifts' are given not only to exercise the particular ministry but also to equip the saints in the work of that ministry *[Ephesians 4:12.16]*. Teams should be made up of people with varied gifts.

• When churches plant daughter churches they are inevitably close at hand. The most needy, distant areas are therefore left untouched. Daughter churches can also so easily be clones of the parent church, and set up so as to be dependent to a greater or lesser extent. Churches should be planted by teams so that they are shaped by the people gifted and experienced to do the work well.

Churches need to be planted by teams so that they are shaped by the people gifted and experienced to do the work well.

• All leaders will recognize the danger of being isolated in times of crisis, without the relationships already built with people competent to help. Churches have seasons of conflict, division, confusion or inertia when the right help can be 'life saving'. Other more positive seasons of transition, leadership appointment or strategic thinking will also benefit from the right input.

Such teams will fill a great need in the life of the local church. They did in the New Testament era, and we are hardly beyond needing what they found so beneficial.

Section Three

The Practice of The Teams

The Team's Relationship to the Churches

The Team's Relationship Together

The Churches' Attitude to the Team

Historical Parallels - William Williams, Pantycelyn

Lessons for Today - 3

Chapter Nine : The Team's Relationship to the Churches

Paul described his relationship to the church in Corinth as that of a spiritual father with his children, *'even though you have ten thousand guardians in Christ, you do not have many fathers, for in Christ Jesus I became your father through the gospel' [1 Corinthians 4:15]*. As a result they were proof of his apostleship, *'even though I may not be an apostle to others, surely I am to you! For you are the seal of my apostleship in the Lord' [1 Corinthians 9:2]*. He describes his ministry to Thessalonica as that of a caring mother, *'we were gentle among you, like a mother caring for her little children. We loved you so much that we were delighted to share with you not only the gospel of God but our lives as well, because you had become so dear to us' [1 Thessalonians 2:7&8]*. With churches he had not founded, such as Rome, he related to them as brothers.

What is more, he and his team did it at great personal sacrifice and at no charge to the churches. There was nothing in it personally for Paul or his team, he was simply obeying God's call. The relationship of the team to the church was essentially one of loving service. They were bond-slaves of a Master who had purchased them, and sent them to plant and care for the church. It was a perspective that kept Paul from any hint of anger, self-pity or regret in the turbulent years of the churches' immaturity. He had committed his life to Christ and His church, *'I face daily the pressure of my concern for all the churches' [2 Corinthians 11:28]*.

His was a role of prayer and care. For Rome he spoke of *'how constantly I remember you in my prayers at all times' [Romans 1:10]*, of Ephesus that *'I have not stopped giving thanks for you, remembering you in my prayers' [Ephesians 1:16]*, to Philippi, *'in all my prayers for all of you, I always pray with joy' [Philippians 1:4], to Thessalonica, 'we constantly pray for you' [2 Thessalonians 1:11]*, and to Colossae *'we have not stopped praying for you' [Colossians 1:9]*. Clearly he made a habit of it, and his spiritual sons followed his lead. Of Epaphras he said, *'he is always wrestling in prayer for you, that you may stand firm in all the will of God, mature and fully assured' [Colossians 4:12]*. He then called the churches to do as he did, to *'pray in the Spirit on all occasions with all kinds of prayers and requests. With this in mind, be alert and always keep on praying for all the saints' [Ephesians 6:18]*.

Of all Paul's letters only that to Titus gives no reference of his praying for them.

His care was deep, detailed and ongoing. *'Besides everything else, I face daily the pressure of my concern for all the churches. Who is weak, and I do not feel weak? Who is led into sin, and I do not inwardly burn?' [2 Corinthians 11:28 & 9]*. His counsel to others was to do the same, *'Keep watch over yourselves and all the flock of which the Holy Spirit has made you overseers. Be shepherds of the church of God, which he bought with his own blood' [Acts 20:28]*. His desire was to see the believers and churches stand and mature : *'We proclaim him, admonishing and teaching everyone with all wisdom, so that we may present everyone perfect in Christ. To this end I labour, struggling with all his energy, which so powerfully works in me' [Colossians 1:8]*. In this process he was consciously setting an example for others to follow, *'therefore I urge you to imitate me' [1Corinthians 4:16]*, *'you became imitators of us and of the Lord; in spite of severe suffering, you welcomed the message with the joy given by the Holy Spirit' [1Thessalonians 1:6]*. A large proportion of his letters was an expression of this care, as were his repeated visits, *'even if I caused you sorrow by my letter, I do not regret it. Though I did regret it—I see that my letter hurt you, but only for a little while— yet now I am happy, not because you were made sorry, but because your sorrow led you to repentance' [2 Corinthians 7:8]*. *'Nothing could be further from the truth than to say that congregations of recent converts were abandoned by the New Testament Evangelists and left to sink or swim. The Evangelists were not only the foundation-layers of the Church, they also watched over the welfare of the congregations that were established.'*[82]

The letters were addressed to the churches, but the issues raised would have been for the particular attention of the leaders. Those whom he mentored developed the same expression of care, *'I hope in the Lord Jesus to send Timothy to you soon, that I also may be cheered when I receive news about you. I have no one else like him, who takes a genuine interest in your welfare' [Philippians 2:19 & 20]*, *'I thank God, who put into the heart of Titus the same concern I have for you' [2 Corinthians 8:16]*. Those he sent to the churches were to encourage as well as inform *[Colossians 4:8, Ephesians 6:22]*. They were to *'strengthen the churches' [Acts 15:41]*, a technical term for establishing and consolidating, so that *'the churches were strengthened in the faith and grew daily in numbers' [Acts 16:5]*. In this prophets had an

82 Alex R. Hay Op.cit page 117

important role as they were to *'encourage and strengthen' [Acts 15:32]*. 'When Paul had started churches his job was not done. He was focused on making them mature in church'.[83] All this involved unstinting hard work. Being a 'messenger' was a matter of costly labour, not flattering status : *'Surely you remember, brothers, our toil and hardship; we worked night and day in order not to be a burden to anyone while we preached the gospel of God to you' [1 Thessalonians 2:9], 'those who work hard among you' [1 Thessalonians 5:12], 'everyone who joins in the work, and labours at it' [1 Corinthians 16:16], 'he almost died for the work of Christ, risking his life' [Philippians 2:30].* Therein lies a distinct difference to many today who take the title 'apostle'.

Inevitably, the team had a greater responsibility when the church was first started than after local leadership had been appointed and had taken responsibility for the day-to-day life of the church. Some have suggested that there was a total break at some point, *'phase-out must be integral to the entire mission agency strategy. It is a comprehensive organizational approach that starts with the end product and works back to those who are responsible for producing it',*[84] though such a policy is at variance with Paul's practice. The policy of Sovereign Grace churches would be more consistent, where like spiritual fathers the team *'enjoys primary responsibility only during a formative season in the local church. After this season, the practical responsibility transfers gradually to the elders of that local church. However mature the church may become, the apostolic team will always retain sufficient responsibility to deal with heresy or immoral leaders. But within a maturing church, the base of responsibility must eventually transfer from the apostles to the elders. When it comes to the leadership and direction of the local church, elders must increase, apostles must decrease'.*[85]

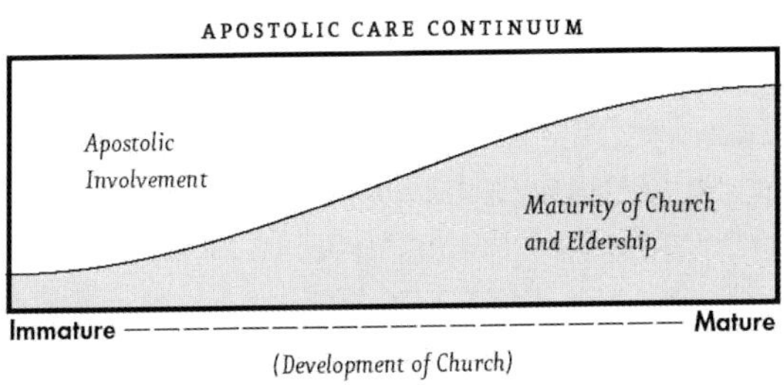

Apostolic Care Continuum [86]

83 Steve Thompson 'Ephesians 4 ministries and church planting'. Private paper.

84 Tom Steffen 'Passing The Baton: Church Planting That Empowers' p.20 quoted in Bernard Lewis's MA thesis

85 Dave Harvey Op.cit page 24

86 Dave Harvey Ibid

As was said earlier, it was not the responsibility of the team to be long-term in a church, or to stay any longer than they had to. *'It was not St Paul's usual practice to establish his fellow-workers as ministers to the infant congregations which he founded'.*[87]

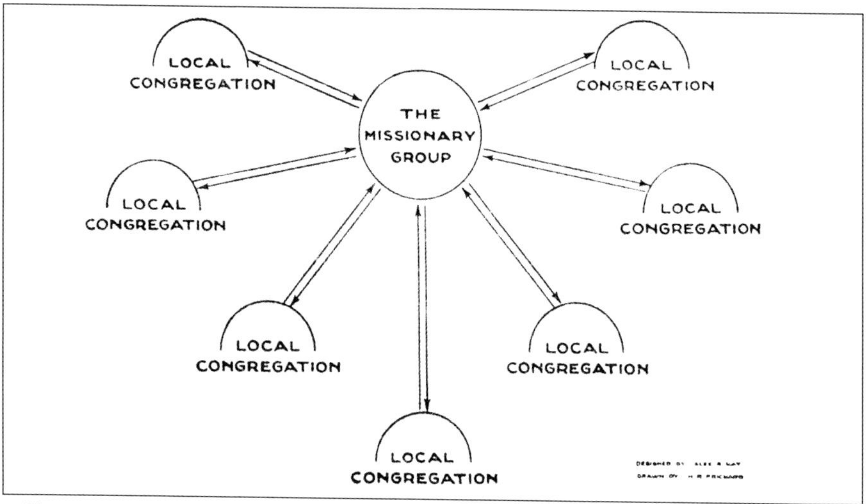

[88]

In terms of the relationship of one church with another the individual churches seem to have had an equal footing. Jerusalem did not hold authority over Antioch once it was established, nor Antioch over Derbe, Iconium or Lystra. The team, however, did have a spiritual authority over the churches they were linked with.

There is evidence to support the notion that different teams served different churches, ***'for God, who was at work in the ministry of Peter as an apostle to the Jews, was also at work in my ministry as an apostle to the Gentiles' [Galatians 2:8]***, and some team leaders may have appeared to have their own following, ***'what I mean is this: One of you says, "I follow Paul"; another, "I follow Apollos"; another, "I follow Cephas"; still another, "I follow Christ"[1 Corinthians 1:12]***. Paul refers to ***'the field God has assigned to us, a field that reaches even to you' [2 Corinthians 10:13]***, meaning the specific areas and churches under his care.

The nature of this authority has been the subject of much controversy, and the justification for 'top down' hierarchies of structured leadership or even

87 Roland Allen 'Missionary Methods' : Lutterworth Press, London 1968 edn. page 86

88 Alex R. Hay Op.cit page 392

'heavy shepherding', as well as the very absence of it. To Barney Coombs the authority of an apostle was a *'governmental input from outside ... interacting relationally and governmentally with the larger body of Christ'* [89] and others have described current charismatic structures as *'governmental but not dictatorial'*, with *'apostolic governance'* having a central role[90]. The same position was held by the Apostolic Church of Great Britain, one of the early Pentecostal groups that arose in the 1920s, especially in its second generation. The apostles were described as the overall leaders of the movement, *'through the General Council of Apostles and Prophets"* [91], *'the founders and rulers of churches...they decided all questions and were the authority'* [92], *'the first and highest office bearers in the church'.*[93] The recognition of men with apostolic and prophetic gifts would seem to be a significant factor in the growth of the Apostolic Church in its first decades through church planting, and subsequently overseas in a mission that vastly outgrew its home base to the present five or six million people. The recognition of gifts parallels the New Testament, but the early emphasis of 'government' does not.

This represents an administrative function in a hierarchy. The problem with such a view is that there is no trace of such a function in the Early Church. Paul had no clear administrative function, no headquarters, and certainly was not a part of a 'council of apostles' who met to direct the work. The Jerusalem 'council' was not a meeting of apostles gathered from a wide area, but of those still in Jerusalem, with the local elders and the church. The teams that Paul led did not represent any form of centralized control.

The teams that Paul led did not represent any form of centralized control.

Paul's authority was a spiritual authority, without an ecclesiastical power to enforce it. Because of his having received his call from the Head of the Church he had, ***'the authority the Lord gave us for building you up rather than pulling you down'*** *[2 Corinthians 10:8]*, but more importantly, because he had founded the church in Corinth he had earned the right to speak authoritatively, even harshly, over incidents of incest, for example, ***'I write***

89 Barney Coombs Op.cit page 176

90 William Kay 'Apostolic Networks in Britain' Paternoster 2007 page 97 & 254

91 'The Apostolic Church - Its Principles and Practices' : Apostolic Publications, Penygroes 1961 page 93

92 James Worsfold 'The Origins of the Apostolic Church of Great Britain'. Wellington, NZ. 1991 Page 82

93 T N Turnbull 'What God Hath Wrought' The Puritan Press Bradford 1959 page 171

these things when I am absent, that when I come I may not have to be harsh in my use of authority – the authority the Lord gave me for building you up, not for tearing you down' [2 Corinthians 13:10]. He could speak in such a way, yet had no human or legal force to support it. He was dependent on God to enforce it. *'The Evangelists were not Bishops or District Superintendents in the modern sense. Their ministry to the churches was governed by different principles. They were not commissioned by the Church but by the Holy Spirit, though their call was confirmed by the Spirit to the Church and recognized by it. Their authority was not ecclesiastical. They had no means of enforcing their judgments. Their authority was purely spiritual'.*[94] His authority was not given by Jerusalem or Antioch, nor by a sending council, nor by other apostles. It came from the Head of the church alone. Paul was not a part, or the pinnacle, of a 'pyramidical' system of church government. The discipline he meted out was entirely spiritual in nature, *'among them are Hymenaeus and Alexander, whom I have handed over to Satan to be taught not to blaspheme' [1 Timothy 1:20].* His scorn at the false apostles of his day, the 'super-apostles' *[2 Corinthians 11:5]*, arose because of the contrast between them in how their ministries were exercised.

When he instructs the churches about marriage he is giving truth that has been revealed to him, and would later be part of the 'revealed truth' of the Scriptures, so he could say, *'this is the rule I lay down in all the churches' [1 Corinthians 7:17].* Because of his relationship with the team members, and because of their loyalty to him and commitment to what God had called him and them to do, he could 'command them', but this was not a kind of military discipline, *'I am sending him to you for this very purpose' [Ephesians 6:27], 'for this reason I am sending to you Timothy, my son whom I love' [1 Corinthians 4:17], 'I am sending him—who is my very heart—back to you' [Philemon 1:12].* His team members had the same kind of authority, *'as I urged you when I went into Macedonia, stay there in Ephesus so that you may command certain men not to teach false doctrines any longer' [1 Timothy 1:3]. 'Authentic apostolic ministry does not begin with an apostle's rights over churches, but with an apostle's calling to serve churches. When an apostle acts "apostolically," his motivation must spring first, not from a positional authority to act, but from a God-given responsibility to serve and a passion to provide care. Emphasizing responsibility as a precursor to apostolic care shifts the historical discussion from the apostle's "rights" to the apostle's "obligations."*

94 Alex R. Hay Op.cit page 124

The shift also fixes the first priority for all apostolic ministry, indeed all Christian leadership – to serve.'[95] *'He had no guarantee of welcome even in the churches he founded. He was forced to argue his case to the church in Corinth and the strength of his case was based more on his relationship to them as father than on his apostolic authority'.'*[96] When he and Barnabas ***'appointed elders for them in each church'*** *[Acts 14:23]*, they were performing a role they had the gifts and experience to do, which the new converts certainly would not have had. When Titus performed the same role, ***'the reason I left you in Crete was that you might straighten out what was left unfinished and appoint elders in every town, as I directed you'*** *[Titus 1:5]*, he did so using the authority and training he had been given.

The attitude of the 'messengers' of New Testament Teams to the churches they are serving, therefore, is critical as to whether their ministry will be received and be on-going. If it is autocratic, controlling or self-serving it will be resisted and rejected. The team has to earn the right to serve by its gifts, wisdom, character, work and credibility. Where, currently, networks seem to offer a 'franchise' to independent churches so that they can join their movement or come under their leadership it is not surprising that they would be resisted as being a 'take-over' and a threat. This is little more than denominationalism under a new guise, but without some of their safeguards. New Testament Teams are to come with a heart to serve, sacrifice and facilitate, with any semblance of authority waiting until relationships, confidences and credibility have been established, and even then it can be refused or ignored by the local leaders. In the case of a church plant, where team members caused the new church to be formed, this confidence and relationship will develop very quickly because the team members are already known and trusted, and their effectiveness and fruitfulness is evident. In these cases where relationships and confidences are growing and the input of the team is being welcomed the new or transitioning church can only benefit.

95 Dave Harvey Op.cit page 21

96 Herbert Harrison Op.cit

Chapter Ten : The Team's Relationships Together

Paul has sometimes been portrayed as a loner, anti-women, and difficult to get on with because of his clash with Barnabas over John Mark *[Acts 15:37-39]*. Nothing could be farther from the truth. He had a remarkable ability to attract people to his team and to work with him, both men and women, as is clear from his contacts in Romans 16 : *'I commend to you our sister Phoebe, a servant of the church in Cenchrea. I ask you to receive her in the Lord in a way worthy of the saints and to give her any help she may need from you, for she has been a great help to many people, including me. Greet Priscilla and Aquila, my fellow workers in Christ Jesus. They risked their lives for me. Not only I but all the churches of the Gentiles are grateful to them. Greet also the church that meets at their house. Greet my dear friend Epenetus, who was the first convert to Christ in the province of Asia. Greet Mary, who worked very hard for you...'.* As quoted earlier, *'Paul attracted friends around him as a magnet attracts iron filings'.*

Paul had a remarkable ability to attract people to his team to work with him, both men and women.

Paul was a gregarious team man. It is touching indeed to see him in Troas, with great opportunities for the Gospel, turning away up the Via Ignatia in search of Titus because he was concerned about him, *'now when I went to Troas to preach the gospel of Christ and found that the Lord had opened a door for me, I still had no peace of mind, because I did not find my brother Titus there. So I said good-by to them and went on to Macedonia' [2 Corinthians 2:12&13]*. Titus was his *'true child' [Titus 1:4]* and *'brother'*. His relationships were so strong that he was troubled and restless in spirit when separated from the team.

His team were not 'delegates' or 'underlings' or 'inferiors', but :

- *'my brother, fellow worker and fellow soldier' [Philippians 2:25]*
- *'fellow worker' [Romans 16:3, 9, 21; 1 Thessalonians 3:2, Philemon 1:23]*
- *'partner and fellow worker among you; as for our brothers, they are representatives of the churches and an honour to Christ' [2 Corinthians 8:23]*
- *'loyal yokefellow ... my fellow workers' [Philippians 4:3]*
- *'fellow servant, who is a faithful minister of Christ on our behalf' [Colossians 1:7]*
- *'dear brother, a faithful minister and fellow servant in the Lord' [Colossians 4:7]*

- *'My fellow prisoner' [Colossians 4:10, Philemon 1:23]*
- *'fellow workers for the kingdom of God' [Colossians 4:11]*
- *'dear friend and fellow worker' [Philemon 1:1].*

This was a very warm, relational, flat leadership structure. They were colleagues working together.

Paul constantly commends, affirms, and encourages the members of his teams. They are described as :

- *'my son whom I love, who is faithful in the Lord' [1 Corinthians 4:17]*
- *'my partner and fellow worker among you ... an honour to Christ' [2 Corinthians 8:23]*
- *'outstanding' [Romans 16:7]*
- *'whom I love in the Lord' [Romans 16:8]*
- *'tested and approved in Christ' [Romans 16:10]*
- *'my dear friend' [Romans 16:9, 12]*
- *'my son whom I love, who is faithful in the Lord' [1 Corinthians 4:17]*
- *'I have no one else like him ... has proved himself' [Philippians 2:20 & 22]*
- *'honour men like him' [Philippians 2:29]*
- *'I vouch for him'[Colossians 4:13]*
- *'respect ... hold them in the highest regard in love' [1 Thessalonians 5:12 & 13].*

In the same way the team members were to actively help and facilitate each other's work :

- *'Do everything you can to help Zenas the lawyer and Apollos on their way and see that they have everything they need' [Titus 3:13]*
- *'the brothers encouraged him and wrote to the disciples there to welcome him' [Acts 18:27]*
- *'They risked their lives for me' [Romans 16: 4]*
- *'they refreshed my spirit and yours also' [1 Corinthians 16:18]*
- *'comforted us by the coming of Titus' [2 Corinthians 7:6].*

Crises over John Mark *[Acts 15:39]* or Phygelus, Hermogenes and Demas *[2 Timothy 1:15; 4:10]* were rare in proportion to the others with whom there was general harmony. The team was held together by the words and actions of all its members.

Whilst on the team there was clearly an 'on the job' training programme. Paul treated the young men as sons and developed, mentored and disciplined them accordingly. Timothy travelled with Paul and then did trips on his behalf, often carrying his letters, and sometimes to places Paul had not visited. Titus went on to develop his own ministry almost independently. Tradition has it that he settled to lead the church in Crete, and his successor

Andreas Cretensis eulogized him as, *'the exalted echo of Paul's own voice'.*[97] Bringing forward the next generation of leaders was clearly central to how Paul saw his role. Frank Viola points out that Paul was in his fifties when doing his journeys, a good age for the period, so the need for succession would be very evident.[98]

Paul's letters to Timothy and Titus were part of this process, when they were away from him. Out of sight was not out of mind when it came to the importance of this task. He was very direct and insistent, *'Timothy, my son, I give you this instruction in keeping with the prophecies once made about you, so that by following them you may fight the good fight...' [1 Timothy 1:18], 'Timothy, guard what has been entrusted to your care. Turn away from godless chatter' [1 Timothy 6:20], 'what you heard from me, keep as the pattern of sound teaching, with faith and love in Christ Jesus. Guard the good deposit that was entrusted to you' [2 Timothy 1:13]*, Paul could confidently say that Timothy knew *'all about my teaching, my way of life, my purpose, faith, patience, love, endurance, persecutions, sufferings' [2 Timothy 3:10]* so he had succeeded in passing on to his deputy what he himself had learned.

It is perhaps worthy of note that Paul 'trained by doing'. There were no theological colleges, seminaries, or training institutions that took people out of the 'real world' into an academic environment for years. Such may well be very valuable, and necessary for some, but Paul's approach should challenge our assumptions, given its effectiveness.[99] *'The recognition of a leadership void has sometimes led to an emphasis on leadership training, producing a leadership elite. This problem can be perpetuated where Bible schools operate independent of local congregations. Even "denominational" Bible schools that take men out of the local congregation run the risk of perpetuating a concept of "qualified leaders" as distinct from mature believers who develop their respective responsibilities'.*[100]

A team without good, honouring relationships would soon be discredited in any church they were serving. Ego, ambition, strife, competitiveness, mutual criticism and undermining would destroy all credibility. The call and the task in hand necessitates the building of strong and enduring friendships among those who would help others.

97 Philip E Hughes 'Commentary on the Second Epistle to the Corinthians' : Eerdmans Michigan 1962 page 76

98 Frank Viola Op.cit page 112

99 Alex R. Hay Op.cit page 488

100 Bernard Lewis Op.cits

Chapter Eleven : The Churches' Attitude to the Team

If it is important that 'messengers' in New Testament teams have right attitudes to the churches and their leadership, then it is equally vital that the churches' attitudes are just as right. The authority of the team has to be earned, and is based on their gifts, influence, integrity and the quality of their relationships. In the same way a right openness and attitude from the church to receive their input should also be built.

Defensive and self-sufficient attitudes will give little room for those with a call to wider ministry to contribute. It is all too common for church leaders, and especially senior leaders, to think that they have to be the mouthpiece that conveys all that God has to say to the church, and to be the one to answer every question and need. 'Who do they think they are coming in here and saying what we should do', can be a sentiment that keeps all outside input at bay, and inevitably leads to inertia and limited vision. Unfruitful traditions are safe where such attitudes hold sway.

Churches are not only encouraged to receive ministry input from the team, but also to assist, facilitate and support that ministry.

The New Testament position is the opposite of this. Churches are not only encouraged to receive ministry input from the team, but also to assist, facilitate and support that ministry. Where the churches had been started by Paul and his team there was an inevitable openness and opportunity to cultivate a right sense of expectation, and even where he had not been responsible for the plant, such as Rome, he still wrote to input, and hoped to visit 'so that I may impart to you some spiritual gift to make you strong' *[Romans 1:11]*. The problems arose when, as in Corinth, other false apostles or legalists came in seeking to undermine his credibility and role.

From the earliest period of the church such input to a church was seen and received as normal. When Jerusalem heard that in Antioch *'a great number of people believed and turned to the Lord' [Acts 11:21]* they sent Barnabas to assess the situation and lay the necessary foundations. To do this he quickly enlarged his team, not from Antioch or Jerusalem but from Tarsus. He brought Paul in and *'for a whole year Barnabas and Saul met with the church and taught great numbers of people. The disciples were called Christians first at Antioch. [Acts 11:26].* The teaching defined them as Christians, and established the right foundations. During this period other ministries came to input into the church, *'some prophets came down from Jerusalem to Antioch. One of them, named Agabus' [Acts 11:27]* and before long a leadership group had emerged including both teachers and prophets, *'in the church at Antioch there were prophets and teachers ... While they were worshiping the Lord and fasting...' [Acts 13:1&2].* Antioch clearly benefited, and became outward looking, giving its prime leaders away for church planting in the nations. There is no suggestion at any point that the initial 'foundation' work was something that they should do themselves. Such would only lead to confusion and a loss of perspective and momentum.

Paul's letters repeatedly lay out the response that the team hopes for and deserves. There were three main areas where a right openness was encouraged.

Firstly, the churches were encouraged to welcome *[Philippians 2:29]* the team members joyfully. In the case of Apollos going to Corinth, *'the brothers encouraged him and wrote to the disciples there to welcome him [Acts 18:27].* To 'welcome' means *'take up, receive, welcome, wait for, expect'*[101] and includes an expectation of hospitality. Timothy's visit to Corinth was to be met by a receptive, accepting, appreciative attitude, *'no one, then, should refuse to accept him' [1 Corinthians 16:11].*

Secondly, this warmth of welcome was to lead to an honouring attitude, *'and honour men like him' [Philippians 2:29].* They were to *'recognize and appreciate properly,'*[102] *'Such men deserve recognition' [1 Corinthians 16:18].* This was to be more than 'being nice', but should lead to a respect that honours the One who sent them, *'he remembers that you were all obedient, receiving him with fear and trembling' [2 Corinthians 7:15].*

Thirdly, it should lead to a willing submission to the authority of the Head of the Church operating through them, *'submit to such as these and to everyone who joins in the work, and labours at it' [1 Corinthians 16:16].* This is not a mindless servility, not behaving like lemmings, but a willingness to be taught, led and corrected. As stated earlier the team had no institutional

101 'The New International Dictionary of New Testament Theology' : Paternoster Press, Exeter 1978 Vol. 3 page 744

102 Charles Hodge '1 & 2 Corinthians' : Banner or Truth Trust Edinburgh 1978 page 371

authority by which they could impose their views, but a spiritual authority by which they expected the Head of the Church to give a conviction in what they said. The word 'submit' means *'to arrange under, to subordinate, to subject ... to submit to one's control, to yield to one's admonition or advice.'*[103] The attitude is best conveyed in Paul's comment on the Corinthians, ***'they gave themselves first to the Lord and then to us in keeping with God's will' [2 Corinthians 8:5].*** *'The apostles could not demand submission and cooperation from the people, but they could receive it from them when it was willingly extended. As the people voluntarily submitted, the apostles led and governed. This is the true pattern for submission and godly authority in the home, the church and the government. A leader cannot lead unless people willingly follow, nor can an apostle demand a response because he is an apostle. Apostles are servants who minister to those who will freely receive their authority.'*[104] *'In all of this cooperation, the apostles' trans-local authority never overrode local authority. The principle of local autonomy and self-rule remained constant.'*[105]

This attitude had a clear benefit on the team as well as the church. When Titus visited he spoke of ***'the comfort you had given him' [2 Corinthians 7:7]***, and that he could see ***'how devoted to us you are. By all this we are encouraged' [2 Corinthians 7:12]***, so that ***'his spirit has been refreshed by all of you' [2 Corinthians 7:13].***

These attitudes were not just to be towards Paul, but also to his team members. Without such an openness and receptivity any team ministry into a church would be unworkable. Once the attitudes and relationships were right benefits not only flowed to the church, but also to the team.

Firstly, the church would pray for the team and the other churches they were involved with, and be aware of the team's plans. Paul was at pains to keep the churches informed of his circumstances and the needs of the churches, ***'I planned to visit you first so that you might benefit twice. I planned to visit you on my way to Macedonia and to come back to you from Macedonia, and then to have you send me on my way to Judea' [2 Corinthians 1:15].***

Secondly, they would provide hospitality for those travelling, ***'if Timothy comes, see to it that he has nothing to fear while he is with you' [1 Corinthians***

103 ὑπο-τάσσω in 'Grimm -Thayer Greek-English Lexicon of the New Testament' page 645

104 David Cannistraci 'The Gift of Apostle' page 150

105 Op.cit page 151

16:10], 'five days later joined the others at Troas, where we stayed seven days' [Acts 20:6]. Later because of itinerants taking advantage of hospitality they could only stay a maximum of two days[106].

Thirdly, they would also be able to help them financially. In Paul's letters it is the impoverished new church in Philippi that was outstanding in this, but presumably others also contributed, *'moreover, as you Philippians know, in the early days of your acquaintance with the gospel, when I set out from Macedonia, not one church shared with me in the matter of giving and receiving, except you only; for even when I was in Thessalonica, you sent me aid again and again when I was in need' [Philippians 4:15 & 16].* It was, however, normal for the team to make no charge to the church they were serving so that they would not leave themselves open to suspicions of their motives, *'what then is my reward? Just this: that in preaching the gospel I may offer it free of charge, and so not make use of my rights in preaching it' [1 Corinthians 9:18], 'I urged Titus to go to you and I sent our brother with him. Titus did not exploit you, did he?' [2 Corinthians 12:18].*

Fourthly, though the churches that originally sent out the team members do not appear to have any on-going responsibility for, or authority over the 'messenger', churches could still participate in the sending process, *'then to have you send me on my way to Judea' [2 Corinthians 1:16], 'no one, then, should refuse to accept him. Send him on his way in peace' [1 Corinthians 16:11].* They were 'in it together'.

Such attitudes and service to the team members would have helped them in their task enormously. It is obvious that real trust and affection developed both ways, *'you long to see us, just as we also long to see you' [1 Thessalonians 3:6].* They further underline the fact that the links between churches and the team were relational and not merely organizational or structural. The New Testament references quoted say much more about the former but little about the latter.

It is obvious that real trust and affection developed both ways.

106 Michael Green Op.cit page 167

Chapter Twelve :
Historical Parallels - William Williams, Pantycelyn

In Chapter Seven the overall fruitfulness of Welsh Methodism was described to show how the principles of 'ministers on the move' worked in the nineteenth century. One of the greatest leaders of this movement will give a good example of how such ministry worked with church groups. William Williams was born in 1717 at Cefncoed three miles from Llandovery in Carmarthenshire, the son of *'a respectable, honest farmer'*. John Williams was one of the ruling elders of Cefnarthen Independent Church, 'a sober, just and quiet Christian'.[107] Williams left home in his late teens to attend the Nonconformist Academy at Llwynllwyd, near Hay-on-Wye, intending to study medicine, but the course of his life was changed forever in 1738. When travelling home he happened to pass Talgarth churchyard as Howell Harris was preaching. In his elegy to Harris he described his preaching :

Come and hear him preach, describing
Man's foul heart - so prone to sin;
Tracing every inward turning,
Full of error, found within;
And disclosing many secrets
To the righteous on their way,
While enlivening death's cold region
With the glorious Gospel ray.

Come and hear him now expounding
Heaven's free, redeeming grace;
Loudly praising the Redeemer
Of our poor apostate race;
Lo! He causes many a pilgrim,
Sore oppressed with fear and grief,
To depart in joyous freedom
From the bonds of unbelief.[108]

He described the effect as a 'a summons straight from glory' to his soul, and says

This the morning, still remembered,
That I first heard heaven's sound;
And the summons straight from glory,
By his voice my heart did wound[109]

I'll not forget the spot, the ground
Where wine flowed
to my soul's foul wounds,
From heaven's store in endless spate,
My wound to heal, my dread, abate.[110]

107 'Trysorfa Ysbrydol', 1813, p. 445; NLW MS 14916A Morgan Williams, 'Llyfr Cofnodion Cefnarthen'

108 Edward Morgan, 'The Life and Times of Howel Harris' : Texas 1998 reprint of 1852 edn. pages.293-4.

109 Eifion Evans, 'Daniel Rowland' Page 62

110 Eifion Evans 'Pusued by God' a selection and translation of 'Theomemphus' by William Williams, : Evangelical Press of Wales 1996 page 17.

He then offered himself for the Anglican ministry and became the curate of Llanwrtyd and Abergwesyn, a remote sparsely-populated area some twelve miles from his home at Cefncoed and just over the border in Breconshire. Howell Harris describes his preaching and its effects, *'my soul was inflamed with love in listening ... The spirit of Brother Rowland is fallen on Brother Williams. O! what earnestness had he! [12 February 1743], 'There came very great power indeed, and there was great crying out' [2 December 1743], 'with him likewise is amazing power' [5 December 1743].* [111]

At the time of his ordination in 1740, or just before, Williams had become a leader in the five or six Methodist societies in the Llandovery area.[112] This and other 'Methodist' activities got him into trouble with the ecclesiastical authorities. His full ordination was refused in 1742, *'on account of his being a Methodist, and going about to preach'*, and this was the year that he was charged in an ecclesiastical court of neglecting his duties in the lesser parishes under his care, and of non-residence. Doors were closing so at an Association meeting in April 1743, with Whitefield as Moderator, the first motion passed among them read simply, *'our Saviour being sought unto for direction, it was agreed that the Reverend Mr. Williams should leave his curacies, and be an assistant to the Reverend Mr. Rowlands'*[113]. This was the decisive moment because it released him to be 'on the move', not 'on the spot'. *'From that time until his death he continued to travel throughout Wales to preach God's message to the darkened inhabitants of the Principality wherever anyone would listen, and he did so for about half a century.'*[114] The impact of this ministry was enormous. In a letter just before his death He claimed he travelled 111,800 miles across Wales preaching and caring for the societies.[115] In a letter to Selina Hastings, Countess of Huntingdon, he said, *'I have promised to write to your ladyship before this, but neglected it by reason of my roving and ranging over the rough mountains and wild precipices of Wales in search of poor illiterate souls chained in the dens of darkness and infidelity.'*[116.]

111 'Cylchgrawn Cymdeithas Hanes Eglwys Methodistiaeth Calfinaidd Cymru' iii.46

112 Eifion Evans 'Pusued by God' page 58

113 'Cylchgrawn Cymdeithas Hanes Eglwys Methodistiaeth Calfinaidd Cymru' xlviii.38

114 Thomas Charles in 'Trysorfa Ysbrydol' 1813, pages 446-7

115 Gomer M Roberts 'Y Per Ganiedydd' : Gwasg Aberystwyth 1949 vol.1 page 164

116 Faith Cook 'Selina, Countess of Huntingdon' : Banner of Truth Trust Edinburgh 2001 page 261

Williams' fame is generally based on his hymns, of which he wrote some 860, such as *'Guide Me O Thou Great Jehovah'.* They had a huge effect on the revival as people sang the truths of the Gospel. Including his hymn books he published over 90 titles, many of which were manuals for Christian discipleship on all kinds of subjects, one *'Drws y Society Profiad'* [The Experience Meeting] was a manual explaining how the society meetings should be run. As he travelled he had a saddlebag of his books and another of tea to sell to cover the cost of his journey.

At the Builth Association on February 1st, 1749 he was put in charge of training the burgeoning number of exhorters, *'agreed that as the brethren stand in need of improvement for their places and work, that till some more effectual means to be found that such as are near and about Llansawel should go there to Mr. Williams either 2 days in the week or a week in the month to improve themselves in grammar, divinity, logic, Philosophy and all knowledge* [and] *to make themselves more useful in their places.'*[117]

Williams was universally described as a man of integrity and good with people. When the emerging Methodist movement split in 1750 due to a clash between Howell Harris and Daniel Rowland it was William Williams who worked tirelessly behind the scenes to effect a reconciliation in 1763. He was a team man who saw the need for unity, harmony and good relationships.

It was his travels to support and order the societies that would have taken most of his time. In an Association Meeting at Trefecca in June 1744 it was *'agreed that Bro. Willm Williams should visit the Societies in ye upper part of Cardiganshire once every six weeks'.*[118] This responsibility widened to cover the surrounding counties in later years, as well as preaching tours to North and across South Wales. His call to assist Daniel Rowland at the Communion services at Llangeitho, where thousands would gather, gives us a snapshot of how he worked. From his home at Pantycelyn, a farm inherited from his mother's family, he would travel through Llandovery and Cilycwm, where he and his wife were members of the society, and up onto the mountains of mid Wales, preaching and visiting societies as he went. Howell Harris had travelled this way to Llangeitho and *'found the people in a most deplorable spiritual condition .... their chief characteristic was a depth of ignorance and apathy that left them only a step removed above the sheep they tended.'*[119]

117 Gomer M Roberts Op.cit page 82

118 Gomer M Roberts Op.cit page 72

119 Hugh J Hughes 'The Life of Howell Harris' : Tentmaker Publications, Hanley 1996 page 98

Harris, Rowland and Williams would preach in farmhouses such as *'Y Fanog'* and *'Rhiwhalog'*, where a society was formed in 1747 which later became the present chapel *'Soar y Mynydd'*, before dropping down to Blaencaron and on to Llangeitho.

In Blaencaron the Society, under William's care, met first at Nantylles and then at Tanyrallt with twenty members in 1742. The minute book at Trefecca for 1744 tells of a visit to the newly formed society at Tanyrallt, led by Dafydd William and Rhys Thomas, *'Tanrallt Society keeps in the fire, the zeal, and its life, and grows in knowledge light and holiness. There are about twenty members, the women being more warm, it is said, than their men. Dafydd William and Rhys Thomas counsel and question them once a week. I myself visit them once in every six weeks, when I hold a private association sometimes, that I may know their doctrine and behaviour. William Williams, 1774.'*[120]

His two key roles as itinerant and hymn writer were mixed together. On one occasion as he faced the congregation, whilst preaching under the oak tree at Tanyrallt, he composed the Welsh hymn[121] :

Cyfliawnder marwol glwyf	The Wounds the law required,
A haeddiant dwyfol loes,	This penalty of pain,
Y pris, y gwerth, yr aberth drud,	The costly sacrifice for sin,
A dalwyd ar y groes,	Demands a Saviour slain.
A gliria 'meiau llwyr,	The debt is fully paid,
A'm gylch yn hyfryd lan;	My sins are washed away,
Ac nid oes arall dan y nef	He only under Heaven,
A'm nertha i fynd ymlaen	Gives strength for that great Day.

The obituary to William Williams in the 'Gentleman's Magazine'[122] in 1791 said, *'in early life a pious but amiable enthusiasm induced him to adopt the itinerant and apostolic modes of Methodism'.* In doing this he demonstrated the invaluable benefits of 'messengers' to a national movement.

120 Gomer M Roberts Op.cit page 88

121 Llyfr Hymnau y Methodistiaid Calfinaidd, No. 482

122 'Gentleman's Magazine' 1791 i. page 91 in 'The Rev Thomas Charles of Bala' by D E Jenkins : Denbigh 1908 vol. 2 page 55

Chapter Thirteen - Lessons for Today - 3

To a very large extent British churches today are focused on their own local efforts or, in many cases, their survival. Calls for a more outward looking stance are often met with a rebuttal on the grounds that the local must first grow large enough to be able to 'give away from strength' or simply that all resources of personnel, time and finance are needed for local struggles. Could it be that such attitudes are one of the causes for decline locally and nationally? Are we not called to *'give and it will be given to you',* and warned that we will reap what we sow? Some churches have, from their beginnings, had a policy of mission and church planting and seem to have prospered as a result.

Church planting studies have shown that churches that do not re-plant in their first five years are unlikely to do so afterwards. It is either built into a church's foundations, its DNA, or it will not happen. Antioch would have had to have other leaders in place before sending Barnabas and Paul but there would never have been a time when they were not seen as 'needed' at home. Leaders of churches, if the principles outlined here are acknowledged as biblical, should build an outward not inward looking culture.

Leaders of churches must build an outward not inward looking culture.

John Wesley certainly did. The influence on England of his preaching, organizing, printing and initiatives for the poor and needy was enormous. For a man whom his enemies called *'Pope John',* he received remarkable respect and loyalty from those who served with him. He inspired, envisioned, trained and released more leaders and exhorters in his generation than anyone else. He records that he held classes and lectures for some of his preachers, his *'assistants'* or *'pupils in the gospel',* gathered for the specific purpose notably at Kingswood School, Bristol.[123] John Telford wrote seven volumes of short biographies of 'Wesley's Veterans' and they were just the well known ones. He published his own books to educate his preachers, edited the works of others, and produced a fifty volume 'Christian Library' over six years to encourage reading. Many of the eight published volumes of his letters were to counsel, advise, direct and correct his preachers. At the end of his life he did not have a natural successor for the

123 John Wesley's Journal for 23 February 1749, Works Bicentennial Edition, Vol. 20, page 263

movement he led, as he had out-lived his peers, so he named a committee of one hundred preachers, the 'Legal Hundred', to take over on his death. As a model of dynamic leadership structure it was not a pattern to copy, for obvious reasons, but it certainly showed his ability to multiply preachers and leaders, as many hundreds of other preachers complained about being left out! He built an extensive team. Church planting and transitioning will fail miserably unless God calls a new generation of leaders and the church inspires, encourages, supports and trains them.

Jesus called us to ***'ask the Lord of the harvest, therefore, to send out workers into his harvest field'*** *[Matthew 9:38]* because the harvest is plentiful but the workers are few. The command and the prospects are still applicable today. Without a vision to raise up a new generation of leaders for 'on the move' as well as 'on the spot' the churches and the people will perish. Paul's vision and enthusiasm made the serving, sacrifice and insecurity seem attractive to young men considering their life's direction. Encouraging young potential leaders to move to plant or transition churches in 'barren areas' will need vision, support and a clear call from the Head of the Church. Leaders without such convictions will not inspire them in others. Planting in adjacent areas, or more to the point where there are already good churches on the grounds of the need for a particular brand or flavour of church, will not address the real needs of the nation. Paul went where new foundations were needed and left the churches to re-plant into their province or region. Without 'New Testament Teams' going first the process is, and will be, largely at a halt.

The implications for change, and challenge, will fundamentally affect the orientation and openness of the local church and the prospects for the nation :

- New models of 'New Testament Team' should be developed from the local churches. These should be based on a culture of serving, sacrifice and trust, not the hierarchical models of the twentieth century that seemed to link to churches on a 'franchise' basis where the team assumed a sense of 'government' over churches.
- Churches should recognize, release and support 'messengers' and 'teams' at all levels, as a conscious act of policy. It does not require legal structures or new denominations, but new relationships, trust, understanding and commitments together. Early Calvinistic Methodism had no legal identity or enforceable structure. Societies or leaders who wanted to link elsewhere were free to do so.

- The relationship between the church and the team will change as their work gets done. They may need to be linked to a church intensively for months or even years to see the adjustments through, but they should not stay. Transitioning to a 'support, counsel and emergency role' should be a goal to be reached as soon as possible so that the team can move on elsewhere.
- Those working together in teams would build friendship, unity, trust and harmony as a priority. Mutual respect is vital. Those leading teams should actively gather team members and do much to affirm, support, train and develop them.
- Local churches, and especially leaders, would recognize and acknowledge their own needs and open their lives and the churches they are responsible for to the input of a team. Doing so is not an admission of failure, inadequacy, or weakness, but good sense and good practice.
- Leaders of local churches or new plants would make a conscious decision to open up their church to the ministry of the team as a positive step forward. Reactions of feeling threatened, insecurity, inferiority or defensiveness should be repented of and resisted.
- Teams coming with the right gifts, experience and attitude are not to be assumed as a source of criticism, but of vital help. They are not a threat or a subtle takeover. Submission to their ministry is a submission essentially to Christ, and then to his servants. If local leaders are uneasy with the developing relationship, input or direction being given, they can end the link and look for resourcing from elsewhere. The autonomy of the local church is not threatened by the team.
- Heart attitudes, in teams or their members, of ambition, empire building, jealousy or competitiveness will destroy the very ministry they are seeking to build.
- Teams would be made up of a variety of gifts, experience and backgrounds. If particular needs are recognized then others can be drawn in with the particular abilities needed. Thus teams are not static or permanent.

Church plants and existing churches that will close if they do not transition to a new model need what New Testament churches needed : input from itinerant, 'on the move' apostolic teams. Without them the prospects for the towns and villages without any Bible believing church are bleak. Sending 'hit and run' teams of students or church members on a week's mission will not plant or build a church. Such initiatives should be within a team's overall plan.

Conclusion

The models and examples in this book have been drawn from the New Testament and illustrated with historical examples of similar practice that produced real benefit in their day. Illustrating from contemporary situations is more problematic because of the suspicion and competitiveness that can exist between the various sectors of evangelicalism. However, there are many current examples where 'ministry on the move' is giving real support to 'ministry on the spot', helping to reverse decline or support the new. I asked one church leader to outline the benefits for his new church. The church plant started with three adults in a front room and after six years the congregation had grown to nearly forty people. A year later it has trebled to over a hundred, including many children and young people.

It's been an amazing spurt of growth and having AB and his team already on board has helped tremendously with some of the challenges and practical aspects of such rapid expansion ... There was passion without agenda for building up the body, and this was key. ... Time, and consistency over time, was a major factor in the development and success of our connection. ... AB's flexibility and availability has allowed his contribution to be greater. He has been released by his church to bring his own unique contribution to other parts of the body and we have been blessed as a result. ... His role is complimentary and relational rather than a formal arrangement. AB has our authority to come alongside our own team to enrich, strengthen and support what we are already doing, for example in the area of discipleship. AB has also introduced other members of his team. One thing we really appreciate is the sensitivity and lack of pressure from AB and his team. Their approach is "how can we help you", not "this is what you should be doing". We cannot stress enough that a strong, long term relationship with AB, coupled with his availability, have been the main basis for our working so successfully together. We recommend similar safeguards to other leaders contemplating such a partnership.

The church in the West needs to see many such examples of growth and support in line with New Testament practice.

If that is to happen there are a number of important questions that will need to be answered :

1. Is the thesis true? Does the New Testament provide a pattern of 'ministry

on the move' beyond that of the Twelve Apostles? If there are biblical grounds for on-going 'lesser apostles' / 'messengers of the churches' then the principle should be taken seriously.

2. Is the pattern relevant? Some practices in the New Testament were culturally conditioned [head coverings, foot washing, kosher meat...]. Is 'ministry on the move', as a concept, relevant for today?
3. How do we work from our current patterns, which we may consider to be sub-biblical, to a more biblical model for the support of new or struggling churches?

Traditions and suspicions may make the prospect of what is outlined here seem quite beyond our reach. However, there may be steps that could be taken to move towards a more biblical expression of mission :

- At very least we should encourage leaders locally, in networks, or denominationally to meet to discuss the three questions above. To fail to do so may mean that we are accepting a 'sub-biblical' practice and so failing our generation.
- Larger churches, groups or networks of churches could consider whether the support and sending of 'ministers on the move' should and could be part of their strategy. They could also consider releasing individuals in their churches to work with 'ministers on the move' in team. Individual leaders may also feel that they should initiate such a process because they themselves are conscious of a call to a ministry wider than the local.
- Leaders with an awareness of national and regional needs should identify locations needing a new plant, or new and struggling churches / plants needing help. Out of such a survey a strategy could emerge. Emerging teams that fit the 'DNA' of those already involved in the plant or church could then begin to build a relationship and ministry link.
- Paul stayed in Ephesus for 18 months but with e-mails, video conferencing, websites and short-haul flights some ministry could be through networking relationally from a distance, with periodic visits for days or weeks.
- Others may feel that the New Testament model described here is calling for urgent and thorough action to see the full pattern introduced immediately through an energetic church planting programme. This is obviously the ideal, but resources will determine its practicality. The primary need will be a supply of equipped church planters with a personal call to a particular area. The lack of this will cause an inevitable delay in nations or regions where church planting has a low profile currently.

What is clear is that *'if we always do what we've always done, we will always get what we've always got.'* Doing nothing, or changing nothing, is simply not an option in most nations in the western world. It is a somewhat ironic fact that we only recognize and call people 'apostles' once they are dead.[124] Mention has been made of people who were described as *'The apostle of Carmarthenshire ... Pembrokeshire ... the North ...'* Other books lie on our shelves describing fruitful and effective preachers and leaders as the *'Apostle of Gower', 'The Apostle of the Peak', 'The Apostle of the North' [Scotland], 'Apostle to Central China' ...* so the shyness to recognize such ministry in the living is not merely a Welsh problem, though it is a problem.

The self evident fact is that we are not effective or functioning in the way that the church in the New Testament did, and have a variety of excuses as to why. Are they valid, or should the church re-examine its roots in case serious omissions have been made? According to Terry Virgo, *'One of God's great provisions to safeguard his church from going astray is a continuing apostolic ministry.'*[125] Paul described the 'messengers of the churches' as ***'an honour to Christ' [2 Corinthians 8:23]***, meaning that *'they reflect his glory'* [Charles Hodge], *'their character is such that it reflects the glory of Christ. He is glorified in them'* [R V G Tasker], *'they were for to him for a name and a praise, who brought glory to Christ as instruments'* [Matthew Henry], *'they have nothing but by Christ's gift'* [John Calvin], *'they will bring the light and victory of the risen Lord into their midst'* [Philip E Hughes]. We need such a manifestation of Christ's glory in the church today.

The essential issue is a question of biblical exegesis and faithfulness. Have theological schemes of interpretation, for very good reasons, or prejudice and suspicion for very bad reasons, closed our minds to what is clearly in biblical text, which is ***'useful for teaching, rebuking, correcting and training in righteousness, so that the man of God may be thoroughly equipped for every good work' [2 Timothy 3:16&17]***? The health of the church, and its effectiveness in the nation, needs an honest and thorough answer followed by obedience, sacrifice, vision and the plans, steps and works of faith.

It goes without saying that without the blessing of God, and a fresh move of the Spirit through the Gospel, no new initiatives will be effective, but a biblical commitment of obedience, faith and sacrifice have always been the response that God uses.

124 Terry Virgo 'Does the Future Have a Church?' : Kingsway, Eastbourne 2003 page 112

125 Terry Virgo 'Restoration In The Church' : Kingsway, Eastbourne 1985 page 160

Bibliography

Allen, Roland 'The Spontaneous Expansion of the Church' : World Dominion Press London 1960

Allen, Roland 'Missionary Methods' : Lutterworth Press, London 1968

Bruce, F F 'The Spreading Flame' : Paternoster Press 1970

Calamy, Edmund 'An Account of the Ministers, Lecturers....who were Ejected' : London 1713

Calvin, John 'Institutes of Religion' : Eerdmans, Michigan 1962

Cannistraci, David 'The Gift of Apostle' Regal Books 1996

Chantry, Walter 'Signs of the Apostles' : The Banner of Truth Trust 1973

Chester, Tim & Timms, Steve 'Total Church' IVP 2007

Connor, Kevin J 'The Church in the New Testament' : City Bible Publishing, Oregon 1982

Connor, Kevin J. 'The Vision of an Antioch Church' : Victoria, Australia 1998

Cook, Faith 'Selina, Countess of Huntingdon' : Banner of Truth Trust Edinburgh 2001

Coombes, Barney 'Apostles Today' : Sovereign Word 1996

Cylchgrawn Cymdeithas Hanes Eglwys Methodistiaeth Calfinaidd Cymru' Vol. XLVIII

Evangelical Movement of Wales 'The Christian Church - a Biblical study' 1966

Evangelical Movement of Wales 'The Ministry and Life of the Christian Church : a basis for discussion'. 1968

Evans, Eifion 'Daniel Rowland' : Banner of Truth, Edinburgh 1985

Evans, Eifion 'Pusued by God' a selection and translation of 'Theomemphus' by William Williams, : Evangelical Press of Wales 1996

Evans, Eifion, 'Calvin's Influence on Mission', Foundations, 48 (Spring, 2002), 4-15.

Grantham, Thomas 'The Successors of the Apostles' 1674 Quoted by Richard Haydon-Knowell in 'Restoration' Magazine Sept. 1985

Green, Michael 'Evangelism in the Early Church' : Hodder and Stoughton 1973

Harvey, Dave 'Polity : Serving and Leading the Local Church'. Sovereign Grace Perspectives Gaithersburg 2004

Hay, Alex R. 'The New Testament Order for Church and Missionary' : New Testament Missionary Union Argentina 1947

Hazell, Keith A 'Will the Real Apostles please stand up' Making Wave Books

Hodge, Charles 1 & 2 Corinthians : Banner or Truth Trust Edinburgh 1978

Hughes, Hugh J 'The Life of Howell Harris' : Tentmaker Publications, Hanley 1996

Hughes, Philip E 'Commentary on the Second Epistle to the Corinthians' : Eermans Michigan 1962

Jenkins, D E 'Calvinistic Methodist Holy Orders' Carnarvon 1911

Jenkins, D E 'The Rev Thomas Charles of Bala' vol.2 Denbigh 1908

Jones, D.D. 'Eglwys Meirion a Hugh Owen in 'Eglwysi'r Annibywyr' yn 'Eglwysi'r Annibynwyr' : Undeb yr Annbynwyr Abertawe 1939

Kay, William K 'Apostolic Networks in Britain' : Paternoster 2007

Kennedy, John 'The Torch and the Testimony' : Gospel Literature Service Bombay 1965

Kingdon, David 'Church Planting in the New Testament' Paper for the 1974 Carey Ministers Conference

Lewis, Bernard MA thesis 'So I Send You' University of Wales Lampeter. 2004

Lloyd-Jones, D Martyn 'Christian Unity'. Banner of Truth. 1980

Malphurs, Aubrey 'Planting Growing Churches in the 21st Century' Baker, Grand Rapids 1992

Morgan, Edward 'The Life and Times of Howel Harris' : Texas 1998 reprint of 1852

Murray, Stuart Church after Christendom Paternoster, 2005.

Murray, Stuart 'Church Planting - Laying Foundations' Paternoster 1998

O'Brien, P.T. 'Gospel and Mission in the Writings of Paul' Paternoster 1995

Rees, D C 'Tregaron, Historical and Antiquarian' : Gomerian Press, Llandyssul 1936

Richards, Thomas 'Wales under the Indulgence' : London 1928

Richards, Thomas Richards 'Wales under the Penal Code' : London 1925

Roberts, Gomer M 'Y Per Ganiedydd' : Gwasg Aberystwyth 1949 vol.1

Robertson, O Palmer 'The Final Word : A Biblical Response to the Case for Tongues and Prophecy Today'. Banner of Trust

Stetzer, EdGrowing Missional Churches' Nashville 2006

Stetzer, Ed'Planting new Churches in a Postmodern Age' Nashville 2003

Stott, John'The Message of 1 Timothy and Titus' BST IVP 1996

Swindoll, Charles R 'Paul, a man of grace and grit' Nelson 2002

The Apostolic Church - Its Principles and Practices' : Apostolic Publications, Penygroes 1961

Turnbull, T N 'What God Hath Wrought' The Puritan Press Bradford 1959

Viola, Frank 'The Untold Story of the New Testament Church' : Destiny Image 2004

Virgo, Terry in Newfrontiers Magazine Volume 2 - Issue 04 - September-November 2003

Virgo, Terry 'Does the Future Have a Church?' : Kingsway, Eastbourne 2003

Virgo, Terry 'Restoration In The Church' : Kingsway, Eastbourne 1985

Wallace, Ronald S. Calvin, Geneva and the Reformation' Nelso 1965

Wallis, Arthur Restoration Magazine September / October 1985

Wesley, John The Works of John Wesley, Bicentennial Edition

White, B.R. 'John Miles and the Structures of the Calvinistic Baptist Mission to South Wales 1649-1660' in 'Welsh Baptist Studies' South Wales Baptist College, 1976

Worsfold, James 'The Origins of the Apostolic Church of Great Britain'. Wellington, NZ. 1991